Building an Autonomous Environment

Building an Autonomous Environment

For Yourself and Your Organization

Jane Frankel

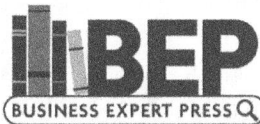

BEP

BUSINESS EXPERT PRESS

Leader in applied, concise business books

Building an Autonomous Environment: For Yourself and Your Organization

Copyright © Business Expert Press, LLC, 2025

Cover design by Charlene Kronstedt

Interior design by Exeter Premedia Services Private Ltd., Chennai, India

First published in 2025 by
Business Expert Press, LLC
222 East 46th Street, New York, NY 10017
www.businessexpertpress.com

ISBN-13: 978-1-63742-776-7 (paperback)
ISBN-13: 978-1-63742-777-4 (e-book)

Business Expert Press Service Collaborative Intelligence Collection

First edition: 2025

10 9 8 7 6 5 4 3 2 1

EU SAFETY REPRESENTATIVE
Mare Nostrum Group B.V.
Mauritskade 21D
1091 GC Amsterdam
The Netherlands
gpsr@mare-nostrum.co.uk

Description

Autonomy is complex. It is independent and dependent. The twenty-first century work requires an autonomous mindset to thrive. Individuals and organizations wishing to thrive will create an environment to enable their autonomy for best decision making. This autonomy includes characteristics of agency, seeing options, and taking control of decisions, all requiring an environment to support them. Valuing and practicing autonomy are essential to thriving in the twenty-first century.

The only competitive force in the twenty-first century that is not matchable by competitors is the members of the organization and their commitment to the vision and mindset of the organization. Organizations need environments that support workers' autonomy and commitment to the organization. This book helps individuals and their organizations build environments that will ensure autonomous and committed mindsets and decisions.

Contents

Preface

Do you want and expect to grow throughout your life? If you, like most, want to grow, how do you want to grow? What must happen in order for you to grow? How will you know if you have grown? Personal and professional autonomy begins with the understanding that development is what leads to growth, and a plan for development is critical to the emergence of growth. Autonomy, or the intentional mindset that fuels strategic decision making and cultivates agency, provides the foundation for growth and leads to the creation of new value. Growth, however, does not happen in a vacuum; networks of individuals and environments form an indispensable foundation of development for the actualization of any initiative.

My first book, *The Intentional Mindset: Data, Decisions, and Your Destiny*, outlined the importance of a mindset–vision alignment to propel the achievement of specifically defined goals. As the first step to this alignment, the understanding of one's own mindset is paramount. In order to enable development, a mindset must be autonomous within the knowledge economy. This book, *Building an Autonomous Environment*, explores the critical aspects of individual behaviors and those of organizations that can inherently support autonomous initiatives through the establishment of shared trust, commitment, and expectations between individuals and their organizations for a structure of autonomy, a culture of growth, and new creation of value. Allow me to share an example of what this could look like.

Serena was a Marketing student at a large university. Her graduation requirement included an internship with a local startup company so that the students would have the chance to build their autonomy and project skills.

Once initiated into the startup, Serena used her skills to gain recognition as a great contributor. Since the company was a small startup, Serena was exposed to the most basic Marketing needs and was charged with responsibility to work autonomously to build a strategic Marketing initiative for the company. She developed multiple projects to expand Marketing efforts to systematically help the company grow. She learned how to identify and target various audiences and how to keep these customers engaged to be assured of their return. Serena enjoyed her experience and became very comfortable with her job, autonomous environment, and continuous learning opportunities.

Once her internship was completed, Serena was offered a full-time position to continue the Marketing work for the small company. She was motivated to stay. Five years later, Serena had grown to become the Director of Marketing for the company that she helped grow with multiple new markets. Both Serena and the company developed and grew together.

There are countless people like Serena who are learning that work becomes meaningful to individuals and to organizations when it autonomously takes control of a specific need, identifies a solution through critical thinking and collaboration, and builds the agency that fosters development and growth for all stakeholders.

Introduction

The concept of the *knowledge economy,* which Austrian economist Peter Drucker (Choong and Leung 2022) named in the 1960s, describes the production of ideas and knowledge from the leveraging of data and information. In contrast with the manual work of farming and then the manufacturing work of industry, knowledge work has become vital to the sustainability of business as accessibility to information has become ubiquitous. As economies evolve from a reliance on agriculture, to a reliance on industry, and finally to a reliance on knowledge, the knowledge economy defines intellectual capital as the ultimate driver of production and services. Previous resources of land, labor, and capital are managed through the intellectual capital of knowledge.

In the United States in the 1930s, when the trend for companies to establish R&D departments emerged, seeds of the knowledge economy were established. It has gained remarkable traction with the introduction of personal computers along with access to the Internet in the 80s and 90s, reflecting the initial shift to what Daniel Bell (1973) defined as a postindustrial society. The knowledge economy relies on the autonomy of workers to leverage the vast amount of information within any particular field and to transform it into valuable advancements.

For the United States, as a developed nation which has the capacity to outsource both agricultural and industrial needs to other agrarian and industry-based economies within developing economies, intellectual capital, or knowledge, represents the most important resource an organization can leverage as it provides the foundation to imagine and create technologies and methodologies that will advance any given industry. In order to thrive within this knowledge economy, both individuals and organizations must embrace a mindset of autonomy to enable latent intellectual capital to manifest. So what is the mindset of an autonomous worker?

Autonomous workers build agency to pursue specific data, information, and knowledge needed to see options for solutions and to make decisions that lead to their successful achievement of new value. Autonomous workers are independently driven to achieve goals and dependently attentive to the needs of their stakeholders. They inquire, collaborate, research, analyze, and make decisions. The management of knowledge as a raw material to fuel new thinking is the primary priority of anyone hoping to thrive within the knowledge economy.

It is clear from data tracking trends in patent applications and approvals that this concept of autonomy has grown as developed nations rely more and more on individuals to be inventors just as much as doers. The steep increase in patent applications indicates the way in which autonomous thinkers are propelling progress, both personally and for their organizations. Over a recent 20-year period, U.S.-issued patents rose from less than 47,642 to more than 168,040 (Powell and Snellman 2004). This trend assuredly suggests an increase in new knowledge along with successful invention as derived from autonomous mindsets.

Autonomous workers consider the essential economic structure of supply and demand in order to ensure that their work is fulfilling a need. This framework makes the work both meaningful and productive in terms of a return on investment of autonomously-driven innovation.

Although autonomy seems to be about the *greater good* for individuals and for organizations, there are some tangible reasons to embrace autonomy in the knowledge economy:

- Autonomous individuals and organizations get to define their achievements with reduced uncertainty.
- Autonomous work is time-saving since everyone is thinking and taking charge of decisions and outcomes.
- Autonomy increases the breadth of new ideas since everyone is expected to be innovative and analytical as often as possible.

My previous book, *The Intentional Mindset,* helps workers understand and build an intentional mindset to enable individual autonomy through the components of goals, values, beliefs, and mode of work. These components support and maintain the autonomous worker's skills of agency, seeking options for solutions to problems, and taking control of decisions. This autonomy also helps build awareness of others' mindsets for facilitating the essential collaborative work of the knowledge economy.

Autonomy:
Agency, Options,
Control

Selfs ensure autonomy and satisfaction.

Self-confidence,
self-accountability,
self-sufficiency

Skills and environment build selfs.

Skills/
Environment

Mindset introduces skills and environment.

Mindset

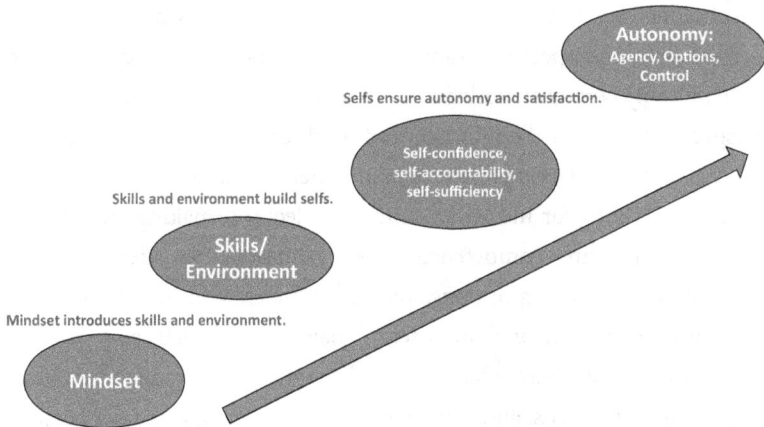

*Figure I.1 **Autonomy***

Figure I.1 describes the progression of thinking needed to build autonomy.

Autonomous skills and a supporting environment provide the benchmarks of autonomy. They complement each other in order to yield the benefits of individual and organizational autonomy in the knowledge economy. Together, they engage and empower individuals to innovate for unlimited development and growth, both for individuals and their organizations.

This book, *Building an Autonomous Environment*, is focused on how you can create the environment to build your own autonomy to develop and grow yourself and for your organization. It is a "How to" book for workers who seek the benefits of being autonomous. Individuals build their own environments for developing their autonomy with the mindset that enables it. Organizations build environments to support those individuals in their pursuit of autonomy, individual development, and the development of the organization.

Autonomy Through Historical Eras

Autonomy combines independence and dependence to allow workers to manage and maximize their work, behaviors, and decisions. Independence comes with worker agency, while dependence helps with finding options for solving problems and taking control of decisions based on all stakeholders' perspectives. Autonomous work considers both economic and behavioral perspectives. Tangible economic perspectives consider the unchangeable factors of work and decision making. Intangible behavioral perspectives consider the mindsets and needs of self and stakeholders.

Autonomy is always present to some extent when working or trading with others, both for individual and joint decision making. Autonomy is defined with three competencies of self-confidence for agency, self-accountability for seeking options, and self-sufficiency for control of decisions. It is enabled by one's mindset of goals, value, beliefs, and mode of work. Levels of autonomy have varied throughout history based on individual mindsets, needs, and extenuating environments. Consider people's mindsets and autonomy in each of these eras:

> *Prehistoric era*—Autonomy led to the individual development and group sharing of tools for hunting and gathering that sustained family life.
>
> *Personalized era*—Autonomy, work, and behaviors were influenced by philosophers, who introduced concepts of good and bad, generosity, benevolence, and sympathy, guiding people's autonomous intentions when working with others (O'Boyle and Welch 2016).
>
> *Classical era*—Autonomy of decisions is based on self-centeredness, personal advantage, and rejecting the personalized approach when trading (O'Boyle and Welch 2016).
>
> *Farming era*—Autonomy of individual expertise in managing the land and its crop output included a high level of knowledge of the agricultural environment and its impact on crops.
>
> *Industrial era*—Autonomy of individual thinking was mostly eliminated as industrialists streamlined work and production processes to maximize factory outputs. Individual workers chose to trade their work efforts and autonomy for money.
>
> *Information era*—Autonomous work included developing the technology needed for identifying and collecting data and information.
>
> *Knowledge era*—Autonomous worker decision making became essential in knowledge work with the challenge of maximizing and utilizing data and information as remote workers with minimal

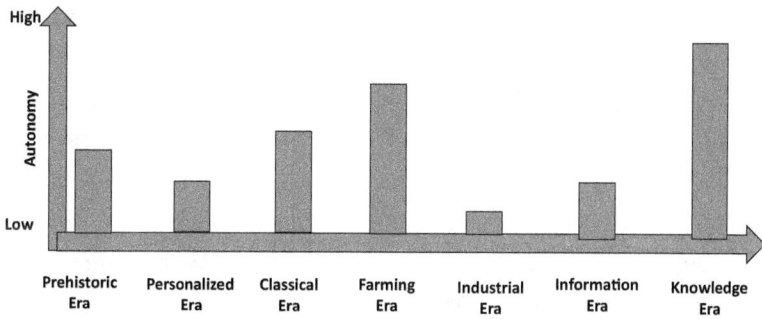

Figure I.2 Estimated Autonomy throughout History

supervisory support. Decisions in this era are influenced by individual and stakeholder mindsets.

Figure I.2 is my speculation on the levels of autonomy through historical eras.

Circumstances along with one's mindset determine a level of autonomy. Let's explore the circumstances of the twenty-first century that have defined its need.

Globalization, Acceleration, and the Knowledge Era

Unlimited access to data and information, remote work, and individual goal setting sounded like a dream come true for Doug. He was eager to take advantage of this environment to be innovative. Doug had just graduated from college and had so many ideas that he had trouble focusing on just one or two of them. He knew that he wanted to work in retail food and local farming. He accepted a position with a food distribution startup where he thought he could use his ideas.

Doug had a strong interest in the food and farm industry, but he didn't really know anything about the systems or details of the providers. His passion was to improve people's health by providing wholesome, nutritious, and fresh foods to those who had no access to them. He majored in Marketing in college, which gave him some great ideas on how to define and expand a market. He was really eager to use these ideas as they applied to food and farms. His new employer was well-funded by a few venture capitalists who saw opportunity in delivering farm fresh food to neighborhoods that had few supermarkets.

Doug's first idea that he shared had to do with daily routine deliveries to corner variety stores for easy customer access. His employer was forced to decline this idea as one of the investors thought it was too expensive to offer this service in so many different locations, even though it would have greatly increased the service Doug envisioned offering these customers. Doug was very disappointed. He had a few other ideas that were also declined due to investors' conflicting interests.

Doug believed in his ideas as they were service-oriented and could be very effective, based on current technology to track and encourage partnerships and sales.

It was time for Doug to become autonomous and use the knowledge economy environment to make his own choices and decisions to build his future. He left his position and started his own venture. He had now met some food and farm workers and customers. He looked forward to building his knowledge of the industry through these acquaintances and considering options for bringing these two groups together to take control and pursue his vision.

The twenty-first century conditions and thinking are as diverse as the number of organizations and knowledge workers that make up society. Challenges abound with the acceleration of globalization, technology, climate change (Friedman 2016), and worker needs. twenty-first century challenges change the landscape of work and workers. Projects take on new contexts, while workers have evolved to want control of their work, their time, and their lives. Workers are also significantly concerned with social issues and contributing to their solutions with their employers. Corporate social responsibility has significantly defined workers' mindsets to shape their work.

These trends require individuals and organizations to address employment, globalization, and acceleration challenges with autonomous work and workers. Challenges include the following:

- ***Worker acquisition, satisfaction, and retention***—requiring trust between organizations and workers to foster development and growth for both
- ***Worker autonomous decision making***—requiring and supporting workers to consider supply and demand factors, build collaborative relationships, and make decisions
- ***Worker creativity for intrapreneuring***—requiring personal development and growth along with creating new value for their organizations
- ***Worker understanding of systems for creating new value***—requiring the context of the organizational and collaborator's mindsets and systems
- ***Joint problem-solving based on various and diverse perspectives*** (Lakoff 2008)—requiring the ability to analyze mindsets and decision factors with critical thinking
- ***Effective understanding and use of artificial intelligence (AI) to facilitate work and decision making***—requiring AI training

Worker autonomy was made especially important by the challenges of the 2020 pandemic and its worker isolation. Generational thinking and the expansion of remote work modified the workplace landscape, creating new modes of work for workers and organizations. As work conditions changed, work became uncertain, and workers were concerned about the future. They became more aware of their desire and ability to be autonomous in their work. They recognized that autonomous independence and dependence could lead to higher performance while increasing their satisfaction with their work. Workers recognized their own strengths and the value of their invisible capital and felt ready to autonomously take control, requiring organizations to accommodate workers' new mindsets and mode of work.

Workforce members had altered their family accommodations, work–life balance, and relationships with co-workers and supervisors. They were not willing to return to the old mode of work. The seeds of autonomy had been planted and would shape workers' mindsets with new requirements for autonomy.

Your invisible capital influences your mindset, which sets up your autonomy
for making independent and dependent decisions.

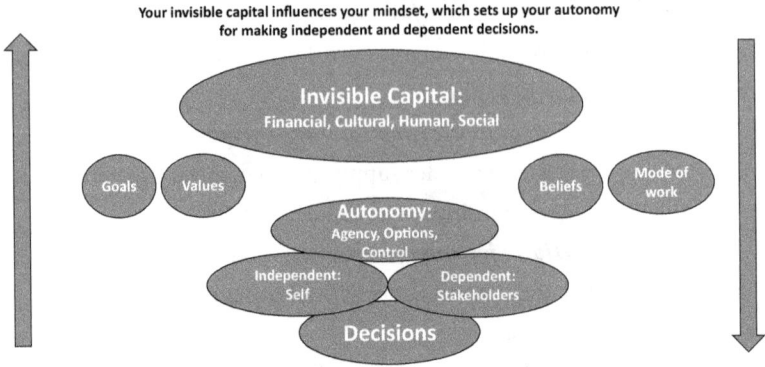

Figure I.3 *Mindset and Autonomy*

Figure I.3 describes how the state of autonomy is built into mindsets, thinking, and decisions.

Fortune's CHRO Daily (2023) publishes regularly on how workers and leaders are managing to face the challenges of today's workplace and environment, citing organizations as they implement new approaches to serving worker needs to build the contentment and motivation of satisfaction and, hopefully, to retain a stable and contributing workforce. These approaches included more frequent reviews, holding conversations as opposed to interviews, and purposeful check-ins on worker well-being.

Autonomy: Knowledge Workers

Building a mindset that understands and builds autonomy is essential. The resulting agency, seeing options, and taking control for decisions alleviates the uncertainty of changing times. Defining the four components of your mindset, being your goals, values, beliefs, and mode of work, is the first step to managing these uncertainties with the certainty ensured by the autonomy of yourself.

> *What might you include in your four mindset components to determine your autonomy?*

Figure I.4 summarizes the rationale and relevance of the four mindset components.

Goals tell what...
your vision with self-sufficiency
Values tell why...
importance with self-confidence, self-accountability
Beliefs tell how...
supporting values with aligned biases
Mode of work tells how, who, and when...
implementing goals, values, and beliefs

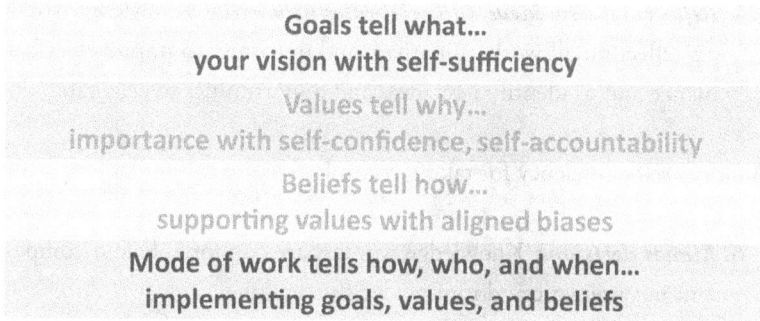

Figure I.4 Mindset Components

A mindset for autonomy is your bible for surviving and thriving. It builds faith and trust in yourself to self-actualize your strengths, knowledge, and skills to achieve your goals. Your autonomy is defined by this mindset.

There are seven skills of autonomy that will help in establishing your agency, seeing options, and taking control of decisions. The following list describes these connections:

Building self-confidence for agency:

1. ***Considers mindsets***: Knowledge workers consider the four components of mindset and their alignment to each other. Mindset considerations happen for each decision and for all stakeholders involved in a work initiative.
2. ***Sets goals and pursues results***: Knowledge workers set goals as part of their work, including a hierarchy of incremental goals and results expected for each effort, including daily work.
3. ***Values inquiry and learning***: Knowledge workers query on all efforts and define expected learning, including exploration of contributing mindsets in support of all efforts.

Building self-accountability for seeking options:

4. ***Ensures data access and uses data for decisions***: Knowledge workers use a digital nervous system (Gates 1999) to support queries with relevant data and information for decision making.

5. *Reflects on new ideas and celebrates new value*: Knowledge workers reflect on all work, initiatives, and outcomes to improve performance and to identify new ideas and opportunities to celebrate.

Building self-sufficiency for taking control:

6. *Makes decisions*: Knowledge workers are comfortable and competent in systematic and routine decision making.
7. *Creates new value*: Knowledge workers systematically pursue improvements and opportunities to create benefits that positively impact themselves and/or their organizations.

Consider a violin protege and how she used her autonomy to self-actualize her goals.

Elena started playing her violin at age 3. She was recognized at an early age as having significant talent and performed at her school and as a soloist with local orchestras. As she grew up, she entered many competitions, making it to the final rounds but usually not winning. She did not progress to the highest stardom, even though that was her goal. However, her love of her music and the violin gave her the perseverance to reconsider her goal and look to her values to find another path to becoming a leader in the music world. She secured a position as a concertmaster of an internationally known orchestra. This position gave her the security of a pay check and the stability of a home to marry and have a family, which were values that she embraced.

Elena brought her talents and work ethic for excellence to appreciating audiences and orchestra peers for whom she provided a role model, support, and an appreciation of excellence. She self-actualized on her own terms and not the terms imposed by others in the music community. She pursued her goals and values in a way that satisfied her passion and vision.

Autonomy gives you the choices of how, what, and when to achieve. It is a gift that you give to yourself within the definition of your mindset. It also allows you to manage the knowledge economy most effectively as you are in charge. The alternative to managing yourself with your autonomy is uncertainty, confusion, and the quiet quitting that accompanies it.

Quiet Quitting

The twenty-first century trend of quiet quitting has relegated approximately 50 percent (Gallup 2022) of workers to a lack of workplace and work engagement, based on over 15,000 full- and part-time U.S. employees surveyed, aged 18 and over. These workers are doing as little as possible to fulfill their work requirements, with no extra effort to develop or grow, for themselves or for their organizations.

Understanding individuals, their mindset, and their needs, as described in personal profiles and development plans, provides insights into their behaviors. Job satisfaction can most assuredly change this trend of quiet quitting by building contentment, motivation, and subsequent satisfaction for quiet committing.

> *Josh, the owner of a landscaping company, noticed that his second and third locations were not as productive as his first location. The revenue at the first location increased 40 percent each year over the last five years. Revenues from locations 2 and 3 remained stagnant during the last two years. All three locations had a few original workers with additional workers hired, as needed. Josh paid workers a percentage of new business revenues based on their referrals. However, there were many more referrals in the first location than in the second and third. He decided to reflect on the differences among all of these locations to identify the cause of the discrepancy in revenue amounts. He started by interviewing his workers. Some were very content but not really motivated to bring in new customers. Others were motivated but wanted a larger cut of the revenue. Had worker contentment caused lack of motivation? What was his next step to be?*
>
> *Josh's workers at locations 2 and 3 were content but not motivated. They enjoyed their work and were paid at a fair rate. They were not feeling motivated to help the business grow, even though they were compensated for referring new customers. They were in need of*

development plans and opportunities to expand their responsibilities and skills to fulfill their development plans.

Quiet Committing

Quiet committing to autonomous work and its results can resolve the quiet quitting trend. I suggest that meaningfulness of work is created through the autonomous mindset that leads to satisfaction. Building satisfaction includes contentment and motivation for development and growth. This committing starts with a mindset focused on building your autonomy. Workers decide through their mindsets what is important to work on, how to work, who to work with, and the goal of this work. An autonomous mindset identifies what you need to be satisfied with your work and commits you to strive for the self-actualization of your strengths toward that satisfaction. Your mindset has created the path of autonomous lifelong learning that will lead to the commitment to reach satisfaction.

Quiet committing requires the environment and resources necessary to support workers' autonomous commitment to their mindsets, others' mindsets, and subsequent work. Understanding individual workers and their needs, as described in personal profiles and development plans, can help managers create the environment that will support workers and their satisfaction.

Josh required each worker to complete a personal profile and development plan to pursue their individual goals. However, he didn't provide an opportunity to fulfill those goals. He determined to create an environment that would have opportunities for his workers.

Autonomous Work in Organizations

Autonomous work balances your mindset with collaborators' mindsets. This management happens through individuals and leaders as they take responsibility for various aspects of work and decisions. Management theories describe how leaders provide structures and environment for work and decision making. Awareness and management of colleagues' mindsets and behavioral tendencies are the domain of individual workers. The learning gained by these management efforts is what actually fuels autonomy.

Management Theories

Three management theories are relevant to autonomous work:

- *Theory X* (Sachs 2022): provides complete direction and guidance for workers on their work, decisions, and goals.
- *Theory Y* (Sachs 2022): expects workers to direct and guide their own work, decisions, and goals.
- *Theory Z* (Quchi 1981): focuses on the well-being and development of the workers.

Leaders and managers shape expectations for autonomous work and workers using various theories as they relate to different scenarios, as well as convey the differing mindsets of the leaders and managers.

Behavioral Tendencies

Diverse mindsets lead to diverse behaviors and decisions. Workers in organizations must be aware of the behavioral tendencies of others, as they impact decisions. These behavioral tendencies are caused by the beliefs included in your mindset. These beliefs or biases translate your values to guide your mode of work. These beliefs and behaviors are described in the newly defined field of behavioral economics. A few psychologists who have contributed to this field include the following:

Daniel Kahneman, author of *Thinking: Fast and Slow* (2011), takes us on a journey of our minds and how we think. Fast thinking happens as a reflex to urgent needs. Slow thinking enables us to process the pros and cons of a situation and make a decision based on this reflection.

Dan Ariely, author of *The Upside of Irrationality* (2011) and *Predictably Irrational* (2009), refutes the belief that our actions are rationale, explaining the hidden reasons that cause behavioral tendencies and their irrationality, as opposed to economically-driven decisions.

Richard Thaler and **Cass Sunstein**, authors of *Nudge* (2009), describe the tools of decision influencers and choice architectures that can help people clarify their thinking and facilitate decisions that may be difficult to make, even though in their best interests.

The field of behavioral economics recognizes and considers the mindsets of members of an economic society. Decisions are impacted not only by the emotions derived from our mindsets but also by the economic logic of rules and regulations put forth by economic theorists. Logic and the emotions of mindsets together guide decisions.

Does your organization facilitate autonomous work?

Learning Organization

Since autonomy is almost completely supported by learning, an organization that expects to support autonomous work will become a learning organization. Peter Senge, author of *The Fifth Discipline* (1990), describes organizational components that will enable workers to be autonomous through learning. Just as individual knowledge workers need to define a mindset that guides their autonomy, the learning organization is dependent upon an organizational mindset that supports autonomy and guides all work and decisions in that context. The learning organizational components include the following:

- *Systems thinking*: seeing the workflow and interdependencies of functions and operations throughout the organization as systems.
- *Personal mastery*: enabling and ensuring that all workers have defined an expertise that is the focus of their individual development and growth.

- *Shared vision*: sharing the organization's vision and mindset with workers for guidance to achievement and work.
- *Mental models*: enabling and ensuring tools, techniques, and protocols to support workers as they embrace the organization's mindset for working on projects and initiatives.
- *Team learning*: enabling and ensuring metrics, tools, techniques, and protocols to guide team activities and learning as a common and continuous mode of work for all teams and their members.

The LEGO (Andersen 2021) has grown to be the largest toy company in the world. It has developed a learning organization very intentionally through the interactions of the founders, employees, and the world around them. The personal mastery, shared vision, and mental models guided employees to reach the highest quality of work and satisfaction with their jobs. Founders created a vision that they shared with their employees, external partners, and customers. Together, the founders and employees were continuous learners through teamwork and frequent innovations.

The Mayo Clinic (Berry and Seltman 2008) touts the first position in the most specialty areas of all U.S. hospitals. They have been serving patients for over 100 years. Dr. William Mayo, its founder, decided to develop the Clinic with his sons, both doctors, into a nonprofit organization with a value of "patients first." Coupling this value with the strategy of integrating medical care, research, and education, the Mayo doctors created an exceptional service organization. The Mayo organization embraces and integrates the five components of the learning organization and environment to provide outstanding service to its patients.

The result of an organization's autonomous environment for knowledge workers is that they can be autonomous in their decision making and innovative in their efforts contributing to their individual and organizational development and growth. Autonomy should be designed to define and achieve the satisfaction of contentment and motivation, so workers and their organizations can maximize the challenges and resources introduced by the knowledge economy.

Building an Autonomous Environment consists of this introduction to the knowledge economy and three sections to guide your reading. The Introduction provides background and a definition of autonomy and its relevance to the knowledge economy. Part I provides a case study and framework for identifying and building your individual autonomy. Part II provides a case study and framework for creating an autonomous environment in your organization. Part III provides insights into reflection on the artifacts and narrative of individual and organizational autonomy. It also provides some thoughts on changing the uncertainty of the twenty-first century to certainties that autonomy and satisfaction can bring. These sections and chapters are described here.

Preface

Introduction

Part I—Building Individual Autonomy

Chapter 1 describes Jill Brown's initiative to build her individual autonomy to self-actualize her talents and goals.

Chapter 2 describes autonomy, learning, and individual satisfaction.

Chapter 3 describes how an individual uses autonomous skills and a learning system (LS) to build and maintain autonomous work.

Part II—Building an Organizational Environment for Autonomy

Chapter 4 describes The LEGO Group as an autonomous organization that demonstrates support, internally and externally, for learning, development, and growth of individuals and the organization.

Chapter 5 describes the components of a learning organization as an autonomous organization.

Chapter 6 describes how to implement the learning organization for building an autonomous environment for individuals and the organization to learn, develop, and grow.

Part III—Checking on Autonomy, Environment, and Satisfaction

Chapter 7 describes the importance and process of reflecting to identify artifacts that lead to your narrative, which validates the autonomy of workers and an organizational environment.

Chapter 8 summarizes how uncertainties can be cured with satisfaction through the autonomy that prompts worker contentment and motivation for surviving and thriving in twenty-first century conditions and challenges.

Autonomy is not really an option in the twenty-first century knowledge economy. So I wish you the best of luck in your endeavors to understand the importance of autonomy in your knowledge work and how to best create the environment to support it for successful outcomes.

PART 1

Building Individual
Autonomy

CHAPTER 1

Building Jill Brown's Individual Autonomy

Jill Brown worked for a large technology company. She was a new technical writer, assigned to an innovative project team. Jim Smith was another team member, who was a supervisor and responsible for overseeing the direction and timeline of the project's work. The purpose of the project was to buy and integrate multiple software tools into one product to shortcut a lengthy development process of designing and building a more comprehensive and larger system.

The project was very complex and challenging as each software tool originated from a different partner company and included diverse partner technology. This larger system was intended to simplify word processing by combining partner tools that included content entry, grammar checks, formatting according to standards, proof reading for alignment of content consistency, and digital document management. Each of these processes was a separate software tool and the new product required them to work together in an integrated manner to create this new and comprehensive word processing system. Word processing tools were new in the technology industry at the time, so this new system would have a great competitive advantage in the business market. The team building this new product was diverse as each process had a unique domain of technology and knowledge. Team members were eager to make one product out of all of the individual ones.

Jill was looking for a leadership opportunity to self-actualize within her own professional development. She felt that she was ready to use her agency, consider options for solutions, and take control of decisions to reach a desired result. She found an opportunity as she observed that the large word processing system was lacking some clarity on the installation and implementation of the larger comprehensive tool.

Installation would be very complex and not yet defined. It also might very well impact the implementation of the overall system. Jill decided to ask some questions about the plans for installation and implementation. The responses she received were not reassuring. This part of the project had not been analyzed or defined. The technology experts were consumed with figuring out how the five tools would be able to work together in a complementary manner, as users would require.

Jill decided that she could contribute to the project by filling this gap in the installation and implementation areas. She decided to explore the feasibility of a solution. She already knew that an installation and implementation solution was urgent, as well as important, to the new word processing system's success. The process for finding a solution would require autonomous work to achieve the result she was pursuing. Once the installation and implementation processes were defined, they would have to be documented for customer use.

Define a Need, a Project, and a Team

Jill's current role on the team was to document the use of this new product for end users. Customer technicians were responsible for installing and implementing the new product. Jill also realized that the new system would not be successful if installation and implementation were unclear. She considered how to solve this need with a new project.

Advocacy

Jill knew that she would need some help with establishing and completing her installation and implementation documentation project. This help would initially involve some advocacy to engage the new product project leaders. Jill set a time to discuss her ideas and proposal with Jim, her colleague on the team. She would like him to act as an advocate for her to help convince the project leaders of the value and importance of her project idea.

Jill and Jim discussed the lack of attention to installation and implementation. He agreed that these needs were critical and would certainly impact the project significantly if not addressed. You cannot sell a product if there are no directions or processes for installing and then implementing it. They understood that the new product had to be installed and implemented to include and integrate all five tools for it to work efficiently and effectively.

Jim agreed to be Jill's advocate to get the project approved. They discussed what research and information they would need to get the project approved. Their first task was to define the needs of all stakeholders who would be involved in contributing and benefitting from the project. This included the project manager, technical experts, customers, company revenue managers, and those who managed the budget for developing the new product.

Project Purpose, Scope, and Desired Result

The purpose of this project was to understand the workflow of the integration of the five tools regarding installation tasks that would set up the implementation of the new product. Their first priority was to understand the need for technical integrations to enable installation and implementation. This inquiry began with the technical experts who were integrating the five tools with each other. These experts had created a few user cases to explore how a customer would use the new product. How did each of these five tools need to relate to each other? What inputs and outputs were dependent upon each other, and in what order were they installed and implemented when a customer would set up the new product?

The desired result of the project was threefold: (1) understand the interdependencies of the separate tools regarding installation and implementation, (2) create installation and implementation programs, and (3) document directions to use these programs.

Idealized Design

Another inquiry was regarding how these installation and implementation processes might change in the future due to updates to any or all of the five tools and their integrations with each other. Looking to the future of potential upgrades would give insights into how the installation and implementation processes would need to be updated and included in the processes and documentation. They engaged the technical experts on each of the five tools to explore possibilities of upgrades.

This inquiry added a fourth desired result, which was to identify potential updates to the installation and implementation processes based on the technologies of the future. One of these future considerations was that end users were becoming more technologically skilled in managing their own systems, installations, and implementations, which would lessen their need for these services.

Define and Build the Mindset Needed

Jim and Jill were very focused on building the project to be successful. They knew that the project manager's attention was overwhelmed with the task of combining the five tools into one workable solution. They would have to be very convincing if they wanted approval to add on to that workload. They cited data on products with installation and implementation processes and documentation and those without, including user success rates for both sets of products.

The need for this new project and team had to be established. A new team would define potential options for designing the installation and implementation processes. This team would test, prioritize, and then select the most feasible option to develop and document. They would use the standard Learning System (LS) that the organization had implemented. It had six consecutive steps that ensured comprehensive and results-oriented work and was familiar to everyone who would participate in their project. These factors would create the mindset to motivate and guide the work of the new project team.

Jill and Jim agreed that the project purpose, scope, desired result, and mindset were focused on benefitting the end users of the new word processing product. The results of the project would also support the company by increasing customer interest to purchase the new word processing product. They also needed to minimize costs so that the installation and implementation systems were feasible to build and service.

They defined the project mindset, including the project's goal, values, beliefs, and mode of work, to guide team members' work and decisions:

Goals

The goal was to create appropriate installation and implementation processes and documentation to satisfy the needs of end users.

Values

Jill defined the project values to be team- and end-user-oriented. They included timeliness, accuracy, data-driven work and decisions, alignment to the team and project charter, and communication protocols for timely sharing of information and work status. Jim and Jill were passionate that their project would ultimately create value for end users.

Beliefs

Beliefs in the value of the project, in the organization and its vision, and in the value of quality and work ethics of the organization were established, along with end-user value to be created.

Mode of Work/Project Charter

Jill considered the timeline of the five tools integration project and determined when the installation and implementation processes and documentation needed to be completed. Jill defined how the work would be completed with a project charter that included:

- Project description with purpose, scope, desired result, and mindset of goals, values, beliefs, and mode of work
- Suggested profiles of team members and their responsibilities for specific domains of expertise
- Stakeholders in the project and its desired result

- Timeline and workplan of the LS steps with incremental goals to be achieved with each step
- Mode of work details
  - Use the seven autonomous skills to facilitate work:
    - Considers mindsets
    - Sets goals for achieving results
    - Values inquiry and learning
    - Ensures the availability of data and information for decision making
    - Reflects on new ideas and celebrates new value
    - Makes decisions
    - Creates new value
  - Budget considerations
  - Decision parameters on ease of use and how installation and implementation processes were designed
  - Tools and research resources available
  - Techniques and protocols to guide decisions, work, and communications
  - Recognition, rewards, and celebration planning
  - Template for sharing information and work status
- Project documentation template to record all project activity and results achieved

Jim and Jill will need to convince the new product project manager to consider their proposal. Once the project charter was completed, Jim prepared the project manager for Jill to discuss it with him. Jim also gathered the project manager's questions so that Jill could respond to them within her presentation and discussion. The proposal was approved, Jill and Jim began to identify relevant team members.

Building the Team

Jill identified and recruited several technical experts who could contribute to the new project as team members. She used the suggested profiles that were included in the project charter to define her search.

With an understanding of the need, technical experts were eager to contribute.

Jill was ready to hold the initial team meeting and present the project charter topics. She distributed the project charter one week prior to the meeting so that team members could review and form relevant questions to ask when the meeting was held.

LS Step 1: Mindset Awareness

Jill ensured that all mindsets were aligned with the project mindset by working through the following steps to build project awareness and alignment. She also allocated significant time for questions so that she could clarify for the team members.

Introduction and Setup

Jill discussed the project charter topics in detail to emphasize the project mindset and common platform for all work, including metrics, tools, techniques, and protocols to be used. Jill included detailed descriptions of this common platform and mode of work that included:

- *Inquiry Structures*—Jill set expectations for inquiry and resulting research. She recognized that asking the right questions was the key to finding data and information needed to enable project work. She coached the team members on three inquiry structures for describing a situation, predicting an outcome, and prescribing a potential solution.
- *Supply and Demand Decision Factors*—Jill coached the team members to use supply and demand formulas of tangible and intangible considerations to manage decision making. Decision-making tools, research, techniques, and protocols were reviewed for use in decision making.
- *LS*—Jill reviewed the six-step LS with the team.
- *Consider Stakeholders' Mindsets*—She also asked team members to consider the mindsets of stakeholders and contributors to ensure that the common mindset was in place to guide all

work. Jill developed a list of all stakeholders and contributors to the project. The team explored the mindsets of all stakeholders and agreed on a path forward to align all mindsets to support the project mindset. Decision influencers and/or choice architectures were used to build alignment. If a stakeholder's mindset match wasn't feasible, Jill recruited a replacement for that stakeholder.

- **Consider Invisible Capital**—Jill identified the invisible capital of her team members, technical experts, and stakeholders. Together with Jim, Jill evaluated each participant's invisible capital and determined how that capital would enhance project work. This capital would contribute to the effectiveness of the team efforts.

- **Explore the Context of Systems**—All work is impacted and influenced by any and all systems involved. The systems of each team member, stakeholder, contributor, and external forces were identified and explored for potential influences or impact to the project work. Accommodation of these systems and their needs is planned.

Aligning Mindsets

Jill and Jim ensured that team members understood the benefits of the installation and implementation processes and documentation as an important service and cost saving for the customer and revenue generating for their own company. Jim and Jill worked to align all mindsets to the project mindset using decision influencers and choice architectures to influence mindsets.

One team member was curious as to why customer technicians would need directions on how to install and implement the new word processing system. He thought that the technical specifications of each tool would be enough information for the customer end users to figure out installation and implementation. Another team member didn't really believe in the value of the comprehensive word processing system, considering the feasibility of integrating five tools into one product.

Jill used market size and projected revenue numbers to estimate the value of the project and the need for installation and implementation and its documentation. She also compared the market share of large products with and without documentation for installation and implementation.

Team members became enthusiastic about participating in the project from one common project mindset. They also agreed to help stakeholders and contributors to adopt this mindset when working on project tasks.

LS Step 2: Entrepreneurial/Intrapreneurial Options for Solutions

Jill led the team to find options to solve the problem of integrating installation and implementation processes.

The team's first task was to define the requirements of a valid option. These requirements would guide the analysis of suggested ideas. Engaging the expertise of each team member, Jill held brain steering sessions to identify the requirements. These analyses were based on the individual characteristics of the five tools being integrated.

Second, Jill held a mind mapping session to identify installation and implementation options that would meet these requirements. Metrics of time, cost to build, and time to install and implement were also applied to the discussion of options.

The team created a list of options, along with their technical requirements, an evaluation of integration and use efforts, and a forecasted result of each option's use to install and implement the product. Jill and the team identified three potential options:

- Install each tool separately and integrate with the previous tools one at a time.
- Combine the tools into one larger tool and install that combined tool all at once.
- Package the tools into technically similar bundles, install each bundle, and integrate to the previous bundles one at a time.

LS Step 3: Economic Analysis

Jill led the team in their economic analyses of the options previously identified. The options are prioritized based on economic feasibility and tangible decision factors of costs and benefits.

The team created the workplan, tasks, and so on, to build each option. Then they estimated the time and cost required for implementing each option, as well as the benefits to be gained.

The team prioritized the list of options based on their economic feasibility:

- *Priority 1:* Combine the tools into one larger tool and install that combined tool all at once.
- *Priority 2:* Package the tools into technically similar bundles, install each bundle, and integrate to the previous bundles one at a time.
- *Priority 3:* Install each tool separately and integrate with the previous tool one at a time.

LS Step 4: Emotional/Mindset Analysis

Jill led the team in emotional/mindset analyses of the options previously identified. These analyses test the acceptance of all stakeholders from the emotional/mindset perspective. These results are added to the results of LS step 3 and prioritized jointly. The option prioritized to be the best option from economic and emotional/mindset feasibilities is implemented in LS step 5.

The team developed a detailed description of each option and the intangible decision factors considered by technology builders and end users. This description included the intangible needs for building, documenting, and using the installation and implementation processes. These descriptions were analyzed in a mind mapping session to evaluate the intangible decision factors of builders and users.

The options were prioritized based on the analysis of intangible decision factors of mindsets and emotions, as follows:

- ***Priority 1:*** Combine the tools into one larger tool and install that combined tool all at once.
- ***Priority 2:*** Package the tools into technically similar bundles, install each bundle, and integrate to the previous bundles one at a time.
- ***Priority 3:*** Install each tool separately and integrate with the previous tools one at a time.

Since LS steps 3 and 4 prioritizations of options were in agreement, priority 1 option was identified as the selected option to implement in LS step 5.

> *Jill, Jim, and team members used their self-sufficiency to take control within LS steps 5 and 6.*

LS Step 5: Implementation

Jill led the team in defining a project plan to implement option 1 as previously concluded.

Jill used the project plan template to define the work and to implement the selected option for creating the installation and implementation processes and documentation. Based on the needs of the selected option, Jill facilitated a brain steering session to identify the steps needed to create the selected option. The project charter mode of work was reviewed to refresh team members' memories.

The team designed, built, integrated, and documented installation and implementation processes for technical and end users to install and implement the new word processing system. The team created:

- A workflow of each tool's installation and implementation steps
- Design of integration programs to combine installation steps and implementation steps
- A workplan for building integrations
- Definition of installation and implementation processes

- Documentation for technical and end-user installation and implementation of the larger tool

LS Step 6: Reflection

Jill led the team in reflecting on actual versus expected outcomes. This reflection considered the benefits and impact of work completed, noting needs for improvement and new opportunities. Each LS step, its work, and its results were reviewed to reflect on potential improvements and to uncover new opportunities.

Jill used the project charter and project summary document to guide discussion on project work, encouraging suggestions on improvements and new opportunities. This reflection also happened as LS steps were completed. Plans were made to initiate any actions needed, such as:

- Improvement in communications between technical experts
- An opportunity to sell installation and implementation services
- Creating a discussion forum for any/all users to keep current on needed updates to the installation and implementation processes

The team was seeking insights into ways to improve work for greater efficiency and effectiveness and for new opportunities for additional value to be created. The team decided to:

- Minimize the time committed to whole team meetings with small and structured discussions
- Create and use a communications template implemented to streamline work and disagreements
- Create an end-user committee to suggest updates and modifications to the installation and implementation programs and documentation

Jill and Jim were both awarded Employee Recognition Awards for their efforts and project outcomes.

Chapter Summary

This chapter provides a description of how an autonomous project was conducted by a technical writer and her advocate. This project explored and built a documentation program that facilitated the installation and implementation of a new and very complex product. The next chapter, "Defining Individual Autonomy," describes the process to develop these autonomous skills and the resources needed to support them.

CHAPTER 2

Defining
Individual Autonomy

As you recall from the Preface, Serena was a Marketing student at a large university. Her graduation requirement included an internship with a local startup company. She was hesitant about the internship because she already had a part-time job with a larger company and the manager wanted her to stay because Serena worked with her so well. Serena liked the manager and was flattered that the manager wanted her to stay. However, Serena's professor insisted that she needed to work independently and dependently, developing her own agency, options for creating new value, and taking control of her work.

The internship proved challenging and Serena couldn't do this job alone. Her aspirations led her to seek out and sometimes even create the organizational resources she needed in order to build her marketing campaign.

As Serena established herself as a contributor and innovative thinker, she developed the Marketing group that not only identified new customers but also new products that these customers would value. There were also new delivery options to be explored, as well as new partnerships to expand that delivery. Serena developed a mindset of endless possibilities for her work and new company. Both Serena and the company grew together.

This chapter describes autonomy, learning, and individual satisfaction. Autonomy includes competencies of self-confidence to build agency, self-accountability to see options for solutions, and self-sufficiency for control of decisions. These competencies drive learning that defines your satisfaction to be achieved by using seven autonomous skills and a learning system (LS) that structures and streamlines work toward a defined goal.

Your mindset defines your individual autonomy and results in your satisfaction with your work and destiny. It specifically defines what satisfaction means to you and how to achieve it. Quiet committing to your mindset goals, values, beliefs, and mode of work will build the satisfaction that you seek.

This all-powerful mindset for autonomy is supported and reinforced by an environment and resources needed to commit to that mindset. Topics include:

- Quiet Committing
- Mindset and Autonomy Defined
- Planning Your Autonomy
- Supporting Concepts of Autonomy
- Checking the Artifacts of Your Autonomy
- Chapter Summary

Quiet Committing

Quiet committing is the solution to resolve quiet quitting. Individuals have defined a mindset that will shape their work to achieve their goals. And their goals define the state of contentment and motivation that will lead to each's satisfaction. A combination of contentment and motivation creates satisfaction. Each worker defines a personal level of contentment and motivation that will add up to the individual's unique satisfaction. This combination may be different at different stages in a worker's life. Worker satisfaction presumes that the workers are autonomous in building their contentment, motivation, and satisfaction.

Mindsets, made up of goals, values, beliefs, and mode of work, build the competencies of autonomy, which will include individual concepts of satisfaction. These competencies of self-confidence, self-accountability, and self-sufficiency lead the way to intentional and continuous learning. Learning creates the path to understanding and pursuing your own contentment, motivation, and satisfaction. So, the autonomous expectations that are included in your mindset can be the frame for your commitment to work and goals to be achieved.

Managers in an organization can commit to understanding worker's individual needs for contentment, motivation, and satisfaction. They then have a roadmap for providing the environment and resources needed for each to reach satisfaction.

Mindset and Autonomy Defined

When I mention autonomy as a mode of work, often I get curious responses. Autonomy has historically meant to work alone. As knowledge economy work is collaborative, in order to fill in knowledge gaps and learn relevant information, we find that others are essential. And as everyone has a mindset with a unique perspective, knowledge workers need to align mindsets to work together. Autonomous work is independent, while it is also dependent. So the important question for doing autonomous work is how do you effectively work with others to achieve a common goal? If you are intent on being autonomous, then you are receptive to understanding your own, as well as other's perspectives and mindsets.

Mindsets determine how and what you think, what you believe, and your mode of work. This mindset begins with your invisible capital of strengths, interest, and experiences and then sets your goals, values, beliefs, and mode of work. Values of inquiry, learning, and trust will prompt belief in a collaborative mode of work that supports autonomy. Individuals and organizations all have mindsets to be considered when working together.

Autonomy is a state of being for individuals and organizations. This state of being is continuously advised by the quest for learning. It maximizes individual and organizational development and growth by empowering, enabling, and motivating workers to collaboratively contribute at the highest levels possible. Every worker is building agency, options/choices, and taking control of work and decisions to maximize individual productivity and organizational performance. Several thinking heads are better than a few. Everyone has the ability to

Using agency:

Know your mindset.

Know your needs.

Build the suppor~ng
environment
to meet needs.

Finding op~ons :

Know stakeholders' mindsets.

Check stakeholders' needs.

List op~ons for mee~ng
all needs.

Building control:

Evaluate op~ons for quality and
quan~ty.

Consider importance, urgency, and
feasibility.

Priori~z e and select the best op~on
for success.

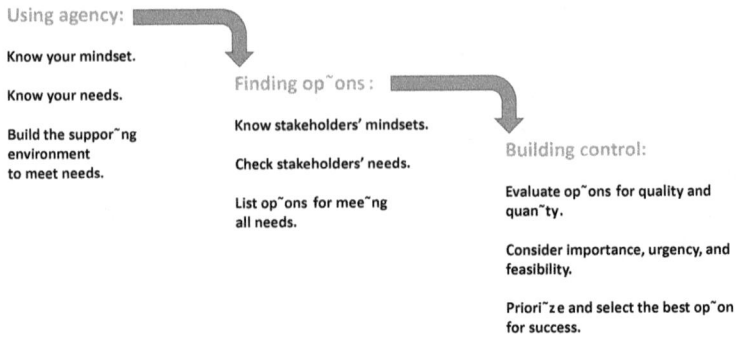

Figure 2.1 Individual Autonomy

inquire, research, analyze, make decisions, improve work, and innovate. Organizations must support these individuals with an autonomous environment to build their autonomy and contributions to the
organization. Figure 2.1 describes the characteristics of autonomy.

Knowledge economy workers, who juggle the twenty-first century
work and requirements, are most successful if they are autonomous in
their work and decisions. Autonomy means that you are independent
in your work as well as dependent on others to complement what
you know yourself. Autonomy (Moore 2016) is defined as having the
agency to take control of your work, behaviors, and decisions. An
additional component of autonomy is the ability to find options for
solving problems. These characteristics also build self-confidence for
agency, self-accountability for seeing options to solve problems, and
self-sufficiency for taking control of work and decisions. All autonomy is
rooted and defined in your mindset.

How does your mindset build your characteristics of autonomy?

*Serena had a definite mindset that valued being employed at all costs
and on others' terms, as needed. She changed that mindset to one of
autonomy when she decided to create her own agenda for success in
the start-up company. She realized that she didn't need a manager
to tell her what to do, she would find great satisfaction in designing
her own path to achieve her own goals, taking advantage of learning*

opportunities along that path. Developing her own mindset of goals, values, beliefs, and mode of work was very motivational.

Building the autonomous mindset sets up the learning that will result in the self-confidence for agency, the self-accountability to find options to solve problems, and the self-sufficiency to take control of decisions to achieve your desired results. This will include working with others and their mindsets.

Building Agency With Self-Confidence

Self-confidence builds your agency to believe that you can navigate mindsets, work, and succeed.

The self-confidence of agency is construed with awareness of your strengths, interests, and invisible capital, which is ascribed to you through nature and nurture or acquired through your efforts and experiences (Rabb 2010). It is all that you know because you have been alive for XX years. Ascribed characteristics may be good looks, your college admission through lineage, or your influential father who makes sure you will have a job upon graduation. Acquired characteristics include your ability to work hard in college and earn A grades consistently, the value you create for your employer, or your network of family and friends who can contribute to your knowledge base.

Recognizing all of these aspects of yourself makes a great foundation for building your agency and self-confidence, which give you belief in yourself to succeed in finding options and in taking control.

> *Your agency builds your self-confidence to be self-accountable to find options and be self-sufficient in achieving your goals.*

Autonomous skills of considering mindsets, setting goals and pursuing results, and valuing inquiry and learning build self-confidence for agency. You are working from a mindset of your power.

Seeing Options With Self-Accountability

Self-accountability enables you to see options to solve problems or take advantage of opportunities. Identifying options takes your agency to the next level, using it to explore various avenues and stakeholders for options that could solve a problem. You are open to all suggestions and not timid in envisioning possible paths. You use the scientific approach to ask relevant questions to explore them. You consider responses to your inquiries as learning, not necessarily as positive or negative.

Your self-accountability sets the foundation for building the self-sufficiency of taking control, which is the third characteristic of autonomy.

Autonomous skills of ensuring access to data and information and reflecting on new ideas and new value build self-accountability for seeing options to solve problems. You are working from a mindset of openness to possibilities.

Taking Control With Self-Sufficiency

Self-sufficiency includes your desire and ability to take control of your work and decisions. It happens when you analyze options based on decision parameters for quantifying, qualifying, and prioritizing them. Your autonomous mindset puts you in control of setting and meeting the parameters that guide decisions and outcomes for success. Your decisions support those parameters.

Your mindset goals, values, beliefs, and mode of work enable these autonomous characteristics. During specific project work, it may be necessary to clarify some aspects of this mindset as relevant to that work. But your basic mindset at the highest level of defining you as a person will always guide your actions, behaviors, and decisions. Clarifications will add another level of details as it is needed to guide a specific project's work. This clarification could be due to considerations of tangible and intangible decision factors/shifters.

Autonomous skills of making decisions and creating new value build self-sufficiency for taking control of work and decisions. You are working from a mindset of persistence in pursuit of value creation.

Elena, a violin protégé, took control of her mindset and shifted her focus to her values as opposed to her goal. She was recognized at a young age as a significant talent in the music industry. As she grew older, she was less competitive and was not a competition winner. She decided to use her passion for the violin but in a different setting than the music industry identifies for young proteges. She shifted her thinking as opportunities presented themselves and found satisfaction in the value she was creating for others, as well as for herself, in her orchestral role as a concertmaster.

Elena's mindset gave her the self-confidence to seek options to fulfill her passion and self-accountability to take control of these options to use her talents to serve others as well as herself.

Figure 2.2 aligns the intentionality and the characteristics of autonomy.

> *How does your mindset set up your autonomous thinking?*

Planning Your Autonomy

Your mindset has four components: goals, values, beliefs, and mode of work. Mindsets determine how and what you think, what you believe, and how you work. It defines your autonomy as it influences your thinking and work. This mindset also defines what will satisfy you as a knowledge worker, which includes your contentment and motivation in your work. Let's explore how these four components of mindset are defined.

Setting Goals

Your vision defines the future of changes and results that you would like to achieve in your specific domain. This vision will drive your work toward your goals and satisfaction. Goals might include specific service to others, achievement of a self-actualizing effort, or building a lifelong

Self-confidence and agency

Self-accountability with finding op°ons

Self-suÿciency f or control

Figure 2.2 Intentionality of Autonomy

environment for success. These goals are the drivers of the remainder of your mindset.

Factors of satisfaction, idealized design (Ackoff, Magidson, and Addison 2008), and your invisible capital will help you define your goals. Satisfaction defines what you need to be content and motivated to create new value. Your satisfaction can be defined within four categories of goals: personal, professional, community, and expertise. Goals in different categories should be complementary and supportive of each other, giving more meaning and support for your overarching vision of the future you would like to create. The satisfaction of contentment and motivation can mean many things to many people as knowledge workers can be complex due to their diverse mindsets. Defining four categories of goals helps to integrate your work for satisfaction as you define your needs. Idealized design and invisible capital are catalysts to defining relevant goals for yourself.

Idealized design defines future needs to impact goal setting. The future speculation of idealized design can assure that your work is not limited by continuous change. Globalization, acceleration, and the knowledge economy present continuous change. Considering how these changes might impact or influence your work, goals, and satisfaction leads to a design of goals that is idealized to accommodate what the future holds. Figure 2.3 describes the formation of an idealized design.

> *Do you have a vision that encompasses the future? Are your goals giving you clarity on your vision? Do your goals also define your values? Is your autonomy one of your goals?*

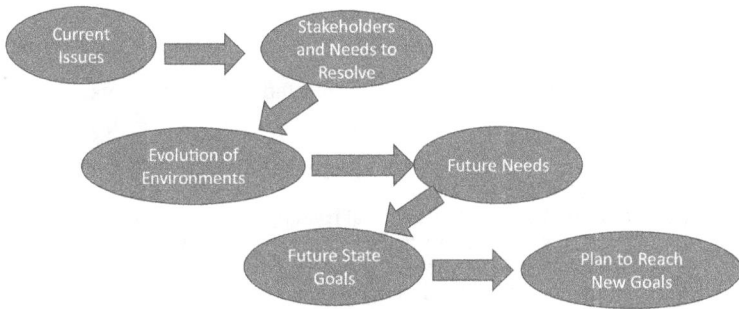

Figure 2.3 Workflow of Idealized Design

Your invisible capital will recognize all of your strengths, interests, and achievements to guide goal setting to maximize your talents. It includes all that an individual knows due to life's nature, nurture, and being alive for XX years, including network of connections, community affiliation, and any other source of your knowledge. Your invisible capital is built through ascribed and acquired factors of your life. After you have identified your invisible capital, you can consider how to take advantage of these aspects to shape your mindset that will guide your thinking, work, and decisions. Figure 2.4 describes the elements of invisible capital.

> *Have you explored your invisible capital? Ascribed? Acquired? Is it included in your goals?*

Finally, consider that goals are oriented toward performance or learning. Learning goals usually support performance goals, as learning precedes performance. Autonomous workers have a combination of learning and performance goals. If goals are all learning, then there is no aspiration to achieve a result. If all goals are performance, the result is achieved with no learning, and learning is imperative in autonomous work.

Goals are the most important aspect of a mindset as they relate to an individual's satisfaction, including contentment and motivation.

Ascribed
- Economic: investments, real estate, production equipment, intellectual property
- Cultural: education qualifications of selected college and degrees

Acquired
- Cultural: programs, curriculums, expertise developed while working
- Human: toolkit of skills, knowledge
- Human: formal education, technical training
- Human: classes, books, informal and formal conversations
- Social: what you know, who you know
- Social: networks of formal and informal groups
- Social: coordination and cooperation for natural benefit

Figure 2.4 Invisible Capital: Economic, Cultural, Human, and Social

Setting Values

Values give context and direction to achieve your goals. They may lead to your goals or may be derived from your goals. In either case, values and goals are aligned to support each other. They are rooted in your analysis of who you are and your strongest characteristics.

Trust is a critical value in creating autonomy. Individuals need to trust their organizations and leaders, while organizational leaders need to trust workers to be autonomous for their best efforts toward organizational goals. Trust can be built by defining and aligning individual and organizational values. When all work, activities, and decisions are made from the same platform of trust, all workers and leaders know what to expect from each other. Workers trust leaders to deliver on the organizational mindset for guiding work, and leaders trust workers to deliver high-quality and results-oriented work toward organizational goals. When trust prevails throughout the organization, productivity and performance are higher than when this trust is in question (Abrams and Burton 2023).

Values of inquiry and learning are also essential to being autonomous. Expectations that all work will include inquiry to yield relevant learning is a key result of agency, seeking options, and taking control of decision making. Autonomy has to depend upon validated facts that are the result of inquiry and learning.

> *Are your values and goals supporting each other? Is building trust one of your values or goals?*

For further consideration on values, Hofstede, Hofstede, and Minkov (2010) researched value dimensions based on the IBM worldwide workforce. They summarized the common values held in various cultures throughout the world of IBM workers. Consider if any of these world values are relevant to you and your autonomous work. These considerations will impact how you approach work decisions. They include:

- *Power distance*: How close to decisions do you like to be? Autonomous workers are comfortable making decisions within their domain of expertise and values, as well as with others making decisions within their domains.
- *Uncertainty avoidance*: How much risk do you tolerate? How do you manage risk?
- *Masculine versus feminine*: Are you aggressive in your approach to work or are you more focused on humanistic tendencies?
- *Individual versus group work*: Do you prefer working individually or working within a team?
- *Long-term versus short-term orientation:* Do you usually focus on short-term or longer-term needs and outcomes?
- *Indulgence versus restraint*: Are you more likely to engage in a new opportunity or take a "wait and see" approach?
- *Other*: Do you have any other tendencies that originate in a value that you hold?

Values of inquiry, learning, trust, and decision-making prompt behaviors in a collaborative mode of work that supports autonomy. Autonomous values might include trust with and for others, learning and inquiry, helping others, inclusivity, recognizing systems that impact yourself and others, belief in other's potential, responsibility for decisions, and always seeing options.

Defining Beliefs

Beliefs are translations of goals and values that guide a mode of work to achieve your goals. These beliefs shape your behavioral tendencies that greatly influence your decision-making. Often these beliefs differ between workers and stakeholders. You might consider your beliefs to be your biases and how they impact your work and decisions. They are neither good nor bad, but they do exist.

Beliefs are important in three ways: (1) recognizing them within your thinking, (2) ensuring that they are aligned with your goals and values, and (3) recognizing them within the behaviors and decisions of your stakeholders. The next important aspect of recognizing your beliefs is the inquiry into why the biases that you have uncovered exist. They are influenced by your values that are derived from your invisible capital of nature, nurture, strengths, interests, and experiences; speculation on the future of external circumstances; and compassion for others.

What are your biases and where did they originate?

Autonomous beliefs might include valuing diversity, inclusiveness, and your unquestioned self-ability. They may also include a tendency to discount other's achievements, their goodwill, or their biases.

Defining Mode of Work

Your mode of work defines how you will apply your values and beliefs to your work to achieve your goals. An autonomous mode of work uses mindsets, metrics, tools, techniques, and protocols to guide decision making.

An autonomous mode of work includes the seven autonomous skills previously discussed. These skills are enabled by the environment and resources needed to support them.

> *What modes of work demonstrate your goals, values, and beliefs?*

A Model for Systematic Development

Workers create a development plan to implement the components of each mindset. Maslow (Smith 2017) defined five stages of human development to reach the autonomy of self-actualization. *These five stages are incremental, and each must be achieved before the next stage can be pursued. They are a framework for developing the contentment and motivation of the satisfaction.* This systematic development is helpful to workers as they work through their development plans to achieve their goals and is also helpful for leaders as they assist workers in their planning and available work opportunities. The stages include:

1. *Physiological needs*: the need for food, water, and compensation
2. *Safety and security needs*: the need for safe, secure habitat, and work environment
3. *Group membership*: the need for group camaraderie, association, and teamwork
4. *Respect as an individual within your group*: the need for recognition within the group, and respect for skills and knowledge
5. *Self-actualization*: the use of your skills and competencies to maximize the value you create and to gain leadership recognition

> *Are your goals self-actualizing? How do your goals and values translate into beliefs that guide your mode of work, decisions, and self-actualization?*

Compatibility of Mindsets

The important question for doing autonomous work is how do you effectively work with others to achieve a common goal. If you are intent on being autonomous, then you are receptive to understanding your own, as well as other's, perspectives and mindsets.

David Brooks (2024a) describes a mindset for collaborating in the context of diverse mindsets. In a *New York Times* opinion column, "Resist the Pull of 'Us vs. Them.'" He suggests middle-of-the-road thinking, being able to alter your individual perspectives in order to reach agreement with those who hold differing perspectives.

The diversity of global cultures in work presents multiple diverse mindsets to consider within autonomous work.

Collaborative Mindsets

Collaborators have mindsets, and they need to be considered along with their systems that impact their work. They include:

- *Stakeholders, Collaborators, and Partners*: Stakeholders are all who can impact your work. Accommodating their mindsets and needs is important to successful collaborative work.
- *Competitors*: Who are your competitors? What are competitors' mindsets and workflow systems and how might they influence your project?

Serena now had a new concept of what would allow her to self-actualize her talents and efforts. She found that she had significant intuition about building a Marketing plan and implementing it. This intuition included building awareness and compatibility of others' needs to engage their support.

Figure 2.5 describes the system for defining your mindset, both individually and as a collaborator.

Supporting Concepts of Autonomy

The concepts of autonomy, which impact mindsets and work, provide context for autonomous work. These concepts include understanding

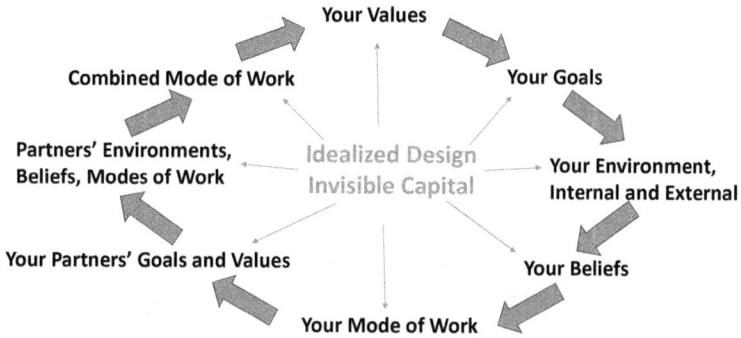

Figure 2.5 Defining a Mindset

systems, supply and demand, skills, learning system, metrics, data inquiry structures, tools, techniques, and protocols.

Systems

Systems consist of inputs and outputs that drive workflow operations. They are the circuits of work aimed at a desired result. The supply chain is a system using several workflows that have interdependence. It works well when all suppliers' and demanders' needs are met throughout these workflows. When supplier and demander levels are complicated by multiple tangible and intangible factors, it is helpful to analyze these workflow systems to identify the workflow inputs and outputs for matches. When the workflows are interrupted, supply and demand may not match.

> *Serena recognized that she knew all about Marketing theory but not necessarily about the actual systems that dictate workflows, behaviors, and decisions. She invested time in researching these systems to know how to meet their needs with her ideas and suggestions.*

Your Mindset System

Your mindset creates a system of your goals, values, beliefs, and mode of work, with each component creating inputs and outputs to each other.

They must be aligned and complementary to work toward your expected result.

Organizational System

The organizational system within which you work is the context for your individual autonomous work. It includes the organizational vision and mindset, all of the workflows of operations throughout the organization, and the mindsets of all collaborators within these workflows. All of these factors will have potential impacts to your work.

Collaborators' and Stakeholders' Systems

Autonomous work is dependent on collaborators and stakeholders. They all have systems within which they work. Understanding these systems is essential to the ability to work with them. Where do they touch your work and each other's work? What is the influence or impact of these connections? Identifying tangible and intangible decision factors within stakeholders' and collaborators' systems of work can be helpful when considering the mindsets involved in decision making.

Systems of External Forces

External forces, such as trends, events, and industry and global needs, all have systems within their domains. Where can you find touchpoints between and among these external forces, their systems, and your work? Are there obstacles, gaps, or tangible or intangible decision factors worth considering?

Awareness of systems and mindsets is motivational since it provides context for helping to align the work of contributors who might differ in their thinking, behaviors, and decisions. Systems and their mindsets create behavioral tendencies. These tendencies are usually caused by beliefs within the collaborators' mindsets. They can be considered obstacles or assets to the project work. Be sure to consider and forecast these behavioral tendencies so you can either integrate them into the project plan or dispel them when needed.

Behavioral Tendencies of Beliefs and Biases

Recently, economists and psychologists have recognized behavioral tendencies that originate from the beliefs and biases that are derived from your goals and values. These tendencies influence decision making and include:

- *Fear of an outcome:* belief in a potential negative outcome
- *Entitlement to something not earned:* belief that one is owed something due to a connection or relationship
- *Overconfidence for achieving a result:* belief in self with no background or experience to support that confidence
- *Narrow framing of a problem:* belief that the very short-term context of a problem is definitive
- *Loss aversion versus appreciation of a gain:* belief that loss is more significant than gain, even if their amounts are the same
- *Confirmation:* looking for validation of what a person already thinks
- *Heuristics:* relying on status quo conditions to make decisions

> *Do you see any behavioral tendencies in your current project?*

Supply and Demand

Decision making can be viewed as a supply and demand equation. Traders maximize their outputs based on their environment, resources, and capabilities to trade with others who have maximized their outputs in the same way. These are the tangible factors that influence trade and decision making, while the mindsets of the traders are the intangible factors that influence trading and decision making. Management of both tangible and intangible factors is the key to autonomous and good decision making. Trading and its decision factors build autonomous work. Understanding the mindsets of your collaborators that lead to their intangible decision factors is essential to making good decisions, as behavioral economists have determined that decisions are most frequently based on intangible decision factors.

> *Decision making and agreement are the same as the supply and demand of trading work, inputs, and outputs. Both are based on logical and emotional decision factors.*

Economic decision factors are tangible, including energy sources, scarcity of materials, productivity, and purchasing power. Mindset decision factors are intangible, including your own and other's mindset perspectives and behavioral tendencies. The ability to manage all of these factors toward a decision that satisfies all collaborators can be complex but not impossible.

Intangible beliefs in the power of free markets or the need for government interventions, the value of humanity, or the value of your own interests are influential in your decisions. These values and beliefs will lead to supply and demand decisions.

> *What do you believe about the collaborators with whom you work and make decisions? What do they believe about you?*

Everyone makes supply and demand decisions as guided by individual mindsets. Consider supply and demand as the catalysts for all collaboration and decision making. Knowledge work is based on the supply and demand decisions of a project's collaborators. Interruptions of timing, resources, or mindset misalignment can break the workflow of decisions that supports work and progress toward a goal. Understanding all decision factors, both tangible and intangible, that can impact this workflow positively and negatively allows the knowledge worker to be in control and reach agreement. Figure 2.6 summarizes autonomous decision making.

Serena built her Marketing activities in the context of customer systems and distribution systems made available through digital

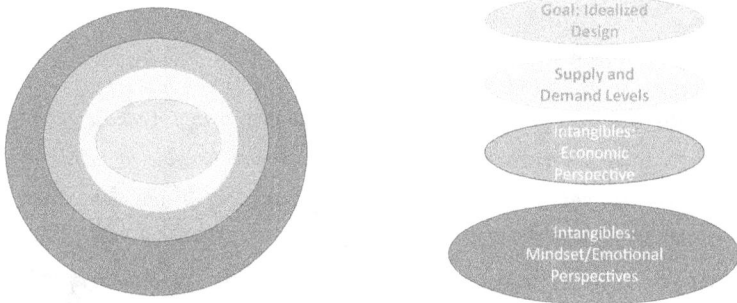

Figure 2.6 Supply and Demand Determinants

connections. She understood how customers could increase their buying and how distributors could expand the geography of her company's sales regions. Serena was attuned to customers' intangible needs and how they would impact their business decisions.

Tangible Decision Factors

Tangible economic factors (Dixon and O'Mahony 2023) are easily defined and calculated and are not easily altered as they are usually beyond the influence of the supplier or demander. Suppliers' tangible factors might include:

- *Cost of inputs*—Has the cost of supplies and materials changed? Does this cost impact, impede, or encourage a different level of supply?
- *Technology*—Has technology or its enablers changed the conditions of production and subsequent supply?
- *Price of other potential output*—Have competitive products and their prices impacted, impeded, or encouraged a different level of supply?
- *Number of sellers*—Has the number or supply competitors changed?
- *Income of sellers*—Has the balance sheet needs of suppliers changed?
- *Excise tax*—Does a potential excise tax interfere with purchases?

- *Subsidies*—Are any government or other subsidies in place to impact, impede, or encourage purchases?

When the cost of wood increased due to a shortage because of a shortage of forest workers, a carpenter may not be able to fulfill a contractual obligation to complete the framing of a new home on time. Since these shortages are universal, that carpenter cannot access wood at another supplier. This is a tangible factor that interrupted supply.

Demanders' tangible factors might include:

- *Income level*—Do demanders' income levels allow purchase?
- *Price of other, similar goods*—Are there similar goods in the market that might distract or deter a demander's purchase?
- *Population of potential buyers*—Are there enough potential buyers to match return on investment needs?
- *Excise tax*—Does a current excise tax interfere with purchases?
- *Subsidies*—Are any government or other subsidies in place to impact, impede, or encourage purchases?

Cost cutting measures prompted a toy manufacturer to switch to plastic for making certain toys, resulting in lower pricing. Customers were drawn to the plastic toys and away from the wooden toys. This is tangible factor that altered demand.

Intangible Decision Factors

Intangible factors (Dixon and O'Mahony 2023) include mindset or emotional motivators that impact supply or demand decisions of all traders. When working to eliminate a gap or an obstacle, solve a problem, or come up with a new idea, intangible factors should be considered. Brainstorming, brain steering, or mind mapping can help to identify the intangible factors of demand or supply decisions.

Intangible factors are often unconscious and are less easily identified than tangible factors and can be resistant to being modified. Analyses of mindsets of all stakeholders can help to identify intangible factors that can be obstructors to a supply and demand match.

Suppliers' intangible factors might include:

- *Expected future price*—Do suppliers perceive a future price that will impact, decrease, or increase supply levels?
- *Return on investment needed*—Does the supplier need a specific level of return on individual investment in the purchase?
- *Trends and events*—Are there global, national, regional, and/or local trends or events that would impede or enhance suppliers' production levels?

School suppliers of paper and pencils anticipate a shortage of materials due to forestry challenges. This shortage will increase their materials' costs and decrease their revenues. They consider price increases to meet their anticipated new costs and become less competitive in their market.

Demanders' intangible factors might include:

- *Preferences*—Are demander characteristics or narratives impacting purchases?
- *Current price*—Is the current price perceived to be too high or too low to make a purchase valid to a demander?
- *Expected future price*—Is there a perceived possibility of a prohibitive future price?
- *Return on investment needed*—Does the demander need a specific level of return on individual investment in the purchase?
- *Trends and events*—Are there global, national, regional, and/or local trends or events that would impede or enhance demanders' purchases?

Toy prices may decline due to a new technological focus on digital games. The obsession with the latest technology developments has altered the demand for best seller toys. This decline in demand has caused the price of the toys to increase due to lower supply created.

Skills of Autonomy

On a daily basis, there are seven skills of autonomy that will propel you to a state of autonomy. They reinforce your agency, seeking options, and taking control of decisions. Using these seven skills will ensure that you develop your autonomy. These skills are described, as follows:

1. *Considers mindsets*: Knowledge workers consider the four components of mindset and their alignment with each other. Mindset considerations happen for each decision and for allstakeholders involved in a work initiative.
   a. *Questions to clarify:*
      i. Who is involved?
      ii. What are their mindsets?
      iii. How do they need to be aligned for project success?
   b. *Resources to support:*
      i. Where will I find mindset information?
      ii. How will I access it?

2. *Sets goals and pursues results*: Knowledge workers set goals aspart of their work, including a hierarchy of incremental goals,and results expected for each effort, including daily work.
   a. *Questions to clarify:*
      i. What are the goals, incremental and final, for this project?
      ii. What are the results expected from each of these goals?
      iii. How and when will I work toward each defined result?
   b. *Resources to support:*
      i. What goals and results are included in the project charter?
      ii. What is the timeline for each of these results to be completed?
      iii. What are the artifacts of each of these results being met?

3. *Values inquiry and learning*: Knowledge workers query on all efforts and define expected learning, including exploration of contributing mindsets in support of all efforts.

a. ***Questions to clarify:***
    i. What background is factual and what is not?
    ii. What questions will clarify the nonfactual background?
    iii. What do I need to know based on these questions?

b. ***Resources to support:***
    i. Where will I find data or information on each of these questions and their answers?

4. ***Ensures data availability and uses data for decisions:*** Knowledge workers use a digital nervous system (Gates 1999) to support queries with relevant data and information for decision making.

    a. ***Questions to clarify:***
        i. What is the realm of concern and influence of this project?
        ii. What data and information are needed and available in these realms?

    b. ***Resources to support:***
        i. How will I acquire this data and information?
        ii. What resources do I need to ensure the acquisition of these resources?

5. ***Reflects on new ideas and celebrates new value:*** Knowledge workers reflect on all work, initiatives, and outcomes to improve performance and to identify new ideas and opportunities to celebrate.

    a. ***Questions to clarify:***
        i. What new ideas have been uncovered?
        ii. How might each be valuable?
        iii. How would each idea contribute to the enterprise and its stakeholders?
        iv. How are these new ideas rewarded?

    b. ***Resources to support:***
        i. What data and information are needed to evaluate each idea?

6. ***Makes decisions:*** Knowledge workers are comfortable and competent in systematic and routine decision making.

    a. ***Questions to clarify:***

      i.   What decisions are imperative to reaching the expected result of the project steps?

      ii. What is the timing of these decisions?

  b. **Resources to support:**

      i.   What data, information, or protocol for decision making is needed?

      ii. How will I acquire relevant resources and approval for making decisions?

7. **Creates new value**: Knowledge workers systematically pursue improvements and opportunities to create benefits that positively impact themselves and/or their organizations.

  a. **Questions to clarify:**

      i.   What are the factors and parameters of new value that are relevant to the enterprise, stakeholders, and the knowledge economy?

      ii. Where might these ideas for new value be uncovered?

  b. **Resources to support:**

      i.   What is the procedure for introducing new ideas?

      ii. How and where are these ideas documented for evaluation?

Using the skills of autonomy provided Serena with the background and context she needed to meet her collaborator's and customer's needs.

A Learning System (LS)

A six-step LS (Frankel 2023a) defines an incremental model for working through a project to structure and align work inputs and outputs. Inputs and outputs are considered in the context of their supply and demand matches. This LS keeps work on track and ensures that a result will be reached. Each step uses the seven autonomous skills to build input to the next step. The steps are interdependent as each relies on the other steps to provide input and define needed output for continuing the project work. The six steps include:

1. *Mindset awareness*: understanding and evaluating mindsets—your own, organization, stakeholders, and the project needs
2. *Entrepreneurial/intrapreneurial options*: finding solutions, options, or opportunities that will solve a problem or create new value
3. *Economic analysis*: quantifying options with economic analysis of tangible decision factors, testing the feasibility
4. *Emotional/mindset analysis*: qualifying options with mindset analysis of intangible decision factors/shifters, testing the acceptance of all stakeholders
5. *Implementation*: defining a project plan and work to implement the workflow of the selected option, integrating all stakeholder systems for context
6. *Reflecting*: considering actual versus expected outcomes for pivoting as needed, identifying the benefits and impact of work completed, and becoming aware of new opportunities

Using Metrics

Define the metrics that will describe success for each step. Be sure to describe the measures to be taken to reach the metric of success. Use the available tools, techniques, and protocols for work and decision making to measure for achieving that metric.

> *Serena always identified a metric that would indicate her success. This metric also gave her context of what she was trying to achieve in each of her Marketing initiatives. She measured the number of customers she needed to get to a level of market share. She measured the amount of additional remote sales she needed to warrant a new distribution partnership.*

Data Inquiry Structures

Some questions that would structure data and information inquiry, research, and analyses include the following:

- What demonstrates goal achievement for each step of your project?
- Who can help with these goals, including suppliers and demanders?
- What is the impact of these goals to each of these stakeholders?
- What might prevent these stakeholders from participating in this project?
- What will incent each stakeholder and collaborator to participate?

These questions and their answers will help you understand stakeholders', collaborators', and partners' decision-making factors. Each step of work will require various inquiry and research needs. A brief description of inquiry types (Davenport and Kim 2013) follows:

- *Describe*: inquiry of economic, behavioral, and management aspects of self, stakeholders, and externalities to identify and describe tangible and intangible factors
- *Predict*:inquiry into the causes and correlations of a gap or obstacle in the supply and demand match to identify economic and behavioral decisions
- *Prescribe*: inquiry into paths to resolve the gaps and obstacles for reaching agreement

Tools, Techniques, and Protocols

Tools facilitate inquiry, research, analyses, and decision-making. Techniques and protocols define how, who, and when to use the skills and tools needed for autonomy. Access to a digital nervous system of data and information; personal and professional profile templates; organizational mindset, structure, and worker inventory; team and project charter templates; analysis and decision-making structures; workflow archetype analyses; communications; and documentation are included as tools, techniques, and protocols for autonomous work. They are described below.

Digital Nervous System

Inquiry, research, and analysis are supported by a digital nervous system (Gates 1999), which is a database of any and all data and information likely to be relevant to your work. It is used to support the work of the LS steps. Examples of digital nervous system data and information include:

- Profiles of collaborators, stakeholders, and partners
- Customer data and information
- Sales data and information
- Operation measures and metrics
- Market and competitor data and information
- Global and industry data and information
- Industry standards for performance
- Competitor and stakeholder profiles and mindsets
- Employee profiles
- Company stories
- Recognition and rewards
- Budgetary context for research and intrapreneuring
- Protocols and parameters for operations and decisions
- Organization vision, mindset, and goals
- Project histories and status
- LS templates and project workplans
- Any other relevant data and information

Also, depending on your stakeholders, you will need data and information resources on specific topics that are relevant to these stakeholders, their systems, and environments. Categories might include, among others:

- Association research
- Government research and databases
- Publications and relevant articles
- Think tank and foundation research

- Partner, stakeholder, and contributor profiles, mindsets, and needs
- Previous project summaries

Consider the specific resources that are available in each of these categories that will be helpful in understanding your stakeholders and their needs. Acquire them, as needed, for each reference during project work.

Serena compiled data on her market, competitors, competitors' purchasing histories, and profiles of all potential stakeholders, collaborators, and partners. This information allowed her to create a plan for meeting their needs when she was ready to work with them. She always knew when to approach a customer, and so on, and get a positive answer to her request.

Professional and Personal Profile Templates

Knowledge workers define their mindsets and their development plans to achieve the goals included in that mindset. A template is available to guide that profile. These profiles are also made available to all organizational members for clarity on all invisible capital within the organization. It includes these topics:

- Mindset of goals, values, beliefs, and mode of work
- Development plan and timeline for meeting goals
- Strengths, interests, networks of connections
- Association memberships
- Community relationships
- Mentors
- Succession and reskilling plan

Organizational Mindset, Structure, and Worker Inventory

The organization's vision, mindset, and structure for supervision and decision making are available for all knowledge workers to reference, along with an inventory of other workers and their profiles. This information provides context for completing all work as it aligns to the organization.

Team and Project Charter Templates

Teams and projects are designed for specific purposes and achievement. A template for guiding this work is available to define, clarify, and streamline efforts to be aligned toward a common mindset.

> *Serena created a team for each initiative, recognizing that using others' talents was a sure path to success. She also defined the team work in a consistent manner using a common template so that all team members were clear on expectations, mode of work, and results to be achieved.*

Analysis and Decision-Making Structures

There are several techniques and tools for identifying relevant factors for decision-making. *Five Whys, Bloom's Taxonomy of Seven Levels of Inquiry, brainstorming, brain steering,* and *mind mapping* are very helpful tools for identifying the relevance of factors toward reaching a desired result.

Five Whys (Serrat 2009) analysis will create an understanding of causes and correlations among gaps and obstacles that are impactful for how and why decisions are made inquiry includes:

1. Why that decision?
2. Why that action?
3. Why that behavior?
4. Why aligned to each other?
5. Why aligned to mindset?

Data and information analysis can also be structured using *Bloom's Taxonomy* (Armstrong 2010) *of Seven Levels of Inquiry* includes:

1. Knowledge of data and information background on a topic
2. Understanding the relevance of that topic

3. Applying that relevance to your project
4. Analyzing individual components of the workflow
5. Synthesizing components to create a new scenario for better value
6. Evaluating the new value to be created with the synthesizing of the components
7. Creating the new value that has been identified

Brainstorming describes the practice in which a high-level and general topic is discussed. Inquiry might include:

Topic: Global Events and Trends
Queries:

1. What are current global events and trends?
2. Which are impactful to our vision and mindset?
3. Where might we connect to an event or trend?
4. What prioritizing of these connections makes sense based on impact, benefit, and cost?

Brain steering describes the practice in which a specific topic is discussed. Inquiry might include:

Topic: Supply Chain Obstacles
Queries:

1. What are the supply chain obstacles?
2. Which are impactful to our vision and mindset?
3. Where might we change to have an impact?
4. What prioritizing of changes makes sense based on impact, benefit, and cost?

Mind Mapping describes the practice in which connections, gaps, obstacles, and new opportunities are uncovered and discussed. Topics might include:

Topic: Removing Supply Chain Obstacles
Queries:

1. Where do we encounter a supply chain obstacle? What does this workflow include?
2. How does this obstacle impact our productivity or performance?
3. What input and output factors might give insight into this obstacle?
4. What change might eliminate the obstacle?

Any of these tools can be used with the others to add more clarity to a topic being researched and analyzed.

Workflow Archetype Analyses

Archetypes are routine workflows that can be evaluated to find causes or correlations of gaps, obstacles, or opportunities within the workflows. The *Five Whys* and *Bloom's Taxonomy of Seven Levels of Inquiry* can connect a gap or obstacle to a stakeholder's unmet needs to uncover the cause or correlation.

There are ten classic archetype models (Senge 1990) to consider when analyzing a workflow, including:

- *Limits to growth:* Accelerating growth is limited due to internal or external response, such as resource constraints or saturation levels leading to negative reactions.
- *Shifting the burden:* Short-term solution lessens the effort toward fundamental long-term corrective measures.
- *Shifting the burden with intervenor:* Same as above but further ameliorates the problem as system members never learn to deal with the problem themselves.
- *Balancing process with delay:* Too much corrective action in response to a delay builds no awareness of progress being made.
- *Eroding goals:* Short-term solution lets long-term, fundamental goals decline.
- *Escalation:* System members or organizations see themselves dependent on building advantage over each other; threatened members escalate their work and offerings to the point of unrealistic outcomes.

- *Success to the successful:* As activities compete for limited resources, successful activities are given more resources than the others, leading to their further success.
- *Tragedy of the commons:* Use of commonly available but limited resources solely for individual use restricts other's use of those resources.
- *Fixes that fail:* A short-term fix has unforeseen long-term consequences that may require more of the short-term fix.
- *Growth underinvestment:* Growth is limited by underinvestment in additional resources as growth reaches its capacity.

When the archetype workflow analysis identifies the cause or correlation of a gap or obstacle, you can design a decision influencer or a choice architecture to help modify a need and decision. Decision influencers include data or information to convince the stakeholder to change a current decision. Choice architectures provide a set of options, each with a likely result, to give the stakeholder in the workflow new rationale for decision making.

An example of an archetype workflow, decision influencer, and a choice architecture follows:

- *Archetype:* eroding goals—short-term action leads to decline of long-term fundamental goals
- *Workflow decision:* controversy regarding use of masks during a pandemic
  - Short-term thinking—violation of individual rights
  - Long-term thinking—limit pandemic infections
- *Decision influencers/choice architectures:* paths to resolution
  - Decision influencers—data and information on infection rates with/without masks
  - Choice architecture—likely infection or not or penalty for non-compliance

Communications

Communications can be of utmost importance to project work or a goal to be achieved. Defining the stages of messages, the audience and their needs, and relevant style for each communication endeavor makes communication effective (Jensen 2000). Stages include the purpose of the message to building readiness, relevance, reinforcing, and reflecting on results of a project. Audience includes an analysis of what a specific group needs to hear when conveying a specific message. Style of communication is essential to be sure that you are communicating in a way that your audience will receive the information being provided.

Documentation

All organizational, individual, and project activities should be documented in specific template formats. It is then made available for all collaborators to assess for background information and use in continuing their contributions to the work. These documentation formats include status updates, activity history, personal profiles, organizational context of vision and mindset, team/project definitions, and results.

Checking the Artifacts of Your Autonomy

Artifacts are the signals of your mindset within your work. They create a narrative of you and your work. Checking on these artifacts is important so that your narrative is what you want others to think of you and your work.

At every LS step, it is worthwhile to check how you are perceived by all stakeholders in your project work. Then, it is possible to make changes along the path of your work if their narrative of you and your work does not match your intent.

An important artifact of your narrative is how you manage your independence and your dependence on other's expertise. How do you align to your values of collaboration and the value of other's expertise? Your narrative is what motivates people to work with you. Since autonomy and knowledge work require independence and dependence, you will want to make others want to work with you. Use these few questions routinely to check on your narrative:

- Did the outcome of a previous project match its mindset?

- Were my decisions well supported by relevant organizational components?
- What stakeholders were impacted by the outcome of my work?
- How did they react to that outcome?
- What was positive and negative about these reactions?
- What would have improved their reactions?
- What new opportunities were uncovered by these reactions?
- What am I looking to achieve?
- Why do I value this result?
- Who else values this result?
- What else do others value in the domain of this result?
- Is there a common goal for my work with others?
- What else do my stakeholders value that I have not considered?
- What do I believe about myself, my work, and my stakeholders?
- How do I work that demonstrates my goals, values, and beliefs?

Serena routinely checked the feedback and sensitivities of her collaborators and customers. She recognized that her impressions of activities and results were not necessarily the same as others held. She was aware that these artifacts needed to match in order to build a narrative that would serve her company well in the marketplace.

Chapter Summary

This chapter defines the concept and components of autonomous work. This autonomy is essential for defining your satisfaction through contentment and motivation for working in the twenty-first century knowledge economy. The next chapter, "Building Individual Autonomy," provides a detailed description of how to implement a project using the concepts of autonomy and a LS to guide a project's work.

CHAPTER 3

Building
Individual Autonomy

Jill, a technical writer, had aspirations of leadership. She saw an opportunity to create a product component that was missing but essential to the project team to which she was assigned. Since she was a newcomer to the company and the team, she knew she would need to be autonomous in her efforts to build and lead a new initiative to create that product component. She made a plan to develop her autonomy as she ventured down the path of creating the initiative.

Autonomy is about you. It is a gift you can give to yourself. Knowing how you think is only part of your success. Knowing how your community thinks is the essential factor in moving toward that success.

When you are autonomous you have developed your sense of agency, can find options to solve problems, and are in control of your behaviors, actions, decisions, and destiny. You are independent and dependent on other resources when needed. And you are clear on the differences.

Your mindset can intentionally guide you to an autonomous existence in any organization within which you work. Managing mindsets, expectations, and decisions is what makes you autonomous. Collaborator and stakeholder engagement from the beginning of an initiative is a critical aspect of autonomous work. Celebrating your joint success solidifies the mindsets of contributors and is essential for all to feel and appreciate the value created. The autonomous worker has developed control of all of this.

Chapter 3 describes the process of becoming autonomous as an individual, using the seven autonomous skills, the learning system

(LS), and required resources needed to support your autonomy. Topics include the following:

- The Essence of Autonomy
- Preparing Autonomous Work on a Project
- Implementing Autonomy with the Project Learning System Steps
- Checking the Artifacts of the Project Narrative
- Chapter Summary

The Essence of Autonomy

The characteristics of autonomy are enabled by competencies of self-confidence, self-accountability, and self-sufficiency. Autonomy is developed and demonstrated through a six-step LS, autonomous competencies, and the application of autonomous skills, as described in Table 3.1.

> *Jill and her associate, Jim, were content with their team assignments for documentation and supervision. They felt competent to fulfill their responsibilities and contribute to the team, as their roles defined. They could have been happy with the current situation and avoided the hard work of defining a new project. However, they were both motivated to add more value to the new product and team. They understood the risk of being content and complacent. They also felt the excitement of self-actualizing their leadership abilities to fill in a gap that would have been devastating to the new product and the organization. They were both feeling a sense of autonomy.*

Planning Autonomous Work on a Project

Autonomous work is most easily developed through a project. Selecting and analyzing a project to define your role, work, and expected results will facilitate autonomy in your work. Complete the following planning for your project using the project charter template, described below:

Table 3.1 LS, Competencies/Characteristics, and Skills

LS Steps	Autonomous Competencies/ Characteristics	Autonomous Skills
Step 1. Mindset awareness: self, collaborators, and stakeholders	Self-confidence and agency	**Considers mindsets:** Knowledge workers consider the four components of mindset and their alignment to each other. Mindset considerations happen for each decision and for all stakeholders involved in a work initiative.
		Sets goals and pursues results: Knowledge workers set goals as part of their work, including a hierarchy of incremental goals and results expected for each effort, including daily work.
		Values inquiry and learning: Knowledge workers query on all efforts and define expected learning, including exploration of contributing mindsets in support of all efforts.
Step 2. Finding entrepreneurial/intrapreneurial options	Self-accountability and finding options	**Ensures data access and uses data for decisions:** Knowledge workers use a digital nervous system (Gates 1999) to support queries with relevant data and information for decision making.
Step 3. Economic analysis		**Reflects on new ideas and celebrates new value:** Knowledge workers reflect on all work, initiatives, and outcomes to improve performance and to identify new ideas and opportunities to celebrate.
Step 4. Emotional/mindset analysis		
Step 5. Implementation	Self-sufficiency and control	**Makes decisions:** Knowledge workers are comfortable and competent in systematic and routine decision making.
Step 6. Reflection		**Creates new value:** Knowledge workers systematically pursue improvements and opportunities to create benefits that positively impact themselves and/or their organizations.

- Project purpose and desired result—What is the need of this project and what benefit will it yield?
  - o Include an idealized design—What future occurrences or future states will impact your work and results? How will those needs be integrated into the project?
  - o Include consideration of invisible capital available—What strengths, interests, and experiences are available within yourself and the organization?
- Define a projected project mindset of goals, values, beliefs, and mode of work—What is the project mindset that will lead to the desired result you are seeking? Are these four mindset components supporting each other?
  - o Goals must be achievable and be connected to your invisible capital of strengths, interest, and so on.
  - o Values must consider and value learning and the work and expertise of others. Determine the values that will support your goals.
  - o Beliefs must have a positive perspective of the stakeholders and matters being considered. Define the beliefs/biases needed to deliver on your goals, values, and project needs.
  - o Mode of work must be inclusive, mindset aware, inquiry-oriented, and recognize the value of reflection and change. Consider the autonomous work skills and the organizational mindset and guidelines for behaviors and decisions.
- Define stakeholders and their systems—Who are the stakeholders and what are the systems and workflows involved that will impact the project?
- Define team members and specific expertise—What expertise and team members are needed to work on this project?
- Evaluate stakeholder and team member mindsets and behavioral tendencies—What are the current mindsets and behavioral tendencies of these potential contributors? Do all have the same goals and values? Do their beliefs support those goals and values? Is everyone working in the same mode with metrics, tools, protocols, and techniques to streamline decisions?

- Define advocacy needed—This advocate is charged with ensuring that the project is supported by all involved and approved, as needed, for continuous autonomous work.
- Define the decision factors of supply and demand—What are the tangible and intangible decision factors of all contributors that will impact work decisions?
- Set metrics—What are the metrics and measures that will determine project success?
- Create a project timeline and meeting schedule—What are the milestones, timing, and goals for each step of the LS?
- Define decision making—What are your decision protocols? Who makes specific decisions and how are decisions made?
- Plan communications, documentation, and templates, as needed—What communications and documentation protocols are needed to support the project?
- What recognition and rewards will be made during and after the project is completed?

Now you are ready to assemble a team and share the project charter with members for their review. Gathering their feedback and refining the project charter will happen in step 1 of the LS.

Implementing Autonomy With the Learning System (LS) Steps

The LS consists of six steps that integrate autonomous skills into each step. Reaching agreement for each step, where supply and demand match, enables work on the next step. Tangible and intangible decision factors must be considered for each step. Using the LS steps as a workplan ensures that your work is focused on the goal, step by step, of your project.

How will all stakeholders align to the common mindset, behaviors, and decisions of the project?

Using the LS also ensures that you are building and reinforcing your autonomy continuously. Figure 3.1 summarizes the alignment of this work.

Building Agency With Self-Confidence

LS step 1 builds your agency. It engages your thinking regarding the most important aspect of your autonomous work, which is being able to identify and match mindsets of all stakeholders for efficient and successful work. This research and analysis builds your self-confidence as you are now prepared to align diverse mindsets into a common mindset that your project will require.

LS Step 1: Mindset Awareness

LS step 1 involves understanding, evaluating, and setting a mindset for your project. Your project requires a common mindset for all contributors. In this step, you share the projected mindset for the project and explore the mindsets of all contributors, compare them, and determine their alignment and impact on the project and each other. This research results in refining the project mindset needed. Project charter discussion might include the following:

- What is the mindset and work needed for the project to be successful?
- How does your own mindset, stakeholders'/team members' mindsets, and the organization's mindset align to that project mindset? Does the project mindset need to be altered?
- What global, national, regional, and local events or trends will have influence on the project? Are these mindsets aligned to your project mindset? Does the project mindset need to be altered?
- What resources do you need to identify all of these mindsets? Are these resources available within your organizational environment? How will you acquire them if they are not currently available?

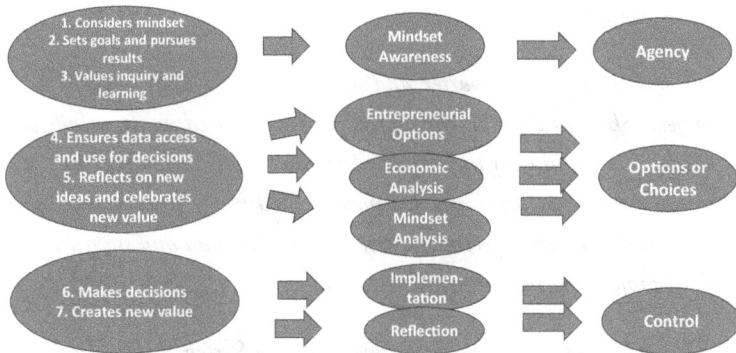

Figure 3.1 Autonomous Skills, LS Steps, and Autonomy

Expected results include the following:

- A project team discusses and refines the project charter and mindset.
- Project charter and mindset differences are identified, and refinements are made, as needed, to align all contributors to the project charter and mindset.
- Discussions, work, and outcomes are recorded in the project documentation.

Resources needed include the following information:

- Stakeholder and collaborator mindsets
- Individual team member profiles, including development and growth planning
- Your own and the organization's mindset
- Data and information on external forces; events, trends, industry protocols, and so on

Worksheet

Create a worksheet to document your mindset research, including the following elements for each contributor and influence to the project:

- Mindset description
- Impact to the project

- Aligning to other mindsets

Jill created a project charter and got approval to launch her new project. She was clear on the project purpose, desired result, mindset needed, and timing of the project. The other topics were less clear, so she speculated on them and planned to modify the project charter, as needed, during project work. She recruited a team and shared the draft project charter for members' review.

Jill began implementing her project with LS step 1 of Mindset Awareness. All team members had to agree on the charter and a common mindset for the project. She also requested team members' help to continuously review all mindsets of stakeholders, collaborators, and partners. This mindset awareness was essential to project success. Jill and Jim would address any misalignment of mindsets so that project work and decisions were expedient and successful.

She reminded the team of the connection of mindsets to goals and results. Inquiry is always a good idea when that connection is unclear.

Jill was now ready to move on the LS step 2 of Finding Entrepreneurial/Intrapreneurial Options to solve the project purpose and problem.

> *Consider your agency, how to measure it, and how it benefits you? How will you use that agency to work through the LS steps?*

Build Your Options/Choices With Self-Accountability

Using your self-accountability to identify, evaluate, and prioritize options further builds your autonomy. This work is focused on options and the feasibility of their economic and emotional/mindsets. LS steps 2, 3, and 4 guide this work.

LS Step 2: Finding Entrepreneurial/Intrapreneurial Options

LS step 2 is focused on identifying potential options and/or opportunities that will solve a problem or create new value. Discussion might include the following:

- What do you wish to solve or create? What is the project's desired result, mindset, and metric to be achieved?
- What are the measures that would lead to or demonstrate this metric?
- What are the parameters for the measures by which to evaluate and prioritize these components or elements, including stakeholder mindsets?
- Who and what are the critical solution components or elements that could contribute to these measures?
- Do stakeholder mindsets align to create these solution components? Do mindsets need to be altered?
- Use research results to identify feasible options for reaching the desired result.

Expected results include the following:

- A list of feasible options is created for solving the project's problem.
- Options are aligned to the mindset and desired result defined in LS step 1.
- Discussions, work, and outcomes are recorded in the project documentation.

Resources needed include the following:

- Data and information on global, industry, competitor, and partner trends and events
- *Brainstorming, brain steering, mind mapping, Five Whys*, and *Bloom's Taxonomy of Seven Levels of Inquiry* templates and discussions

- Parameters for acceptable ranges of metrics, measures, and desired results
- Metrics and measures for evaluating options

Worksheet

Create a worksheet to document your options research, including the following topics for each option:

- Mindset defined
- Goals and results
- Inquiry types (*brainstorming*, etc.,) and learning gained
- Metric and measure parameters.

Jill ensured data and information access and use for decisions. She facilitated reflective discussions on new ideas and celebrated new value uncovered. Jill also reminded the team to consider mindsets, goals, results, and the value of inquiry and learning.

Do you have a list of feasible options to consider in the next LS step?

LS Step 3: Quantifying Options With Economic Analysis

LS step 3 tests the economic feasibility of each option identified in LS step 2. Cost and benefits are evaluated and estimated. Discussions might include the following:

- What product or service defines each option?
- Who are the suppliers and demanders for each option?
- What are the tangible factors of their decisions regarding their economic resources and needs?
- What will each option cost?
- What is the benefit gained from each option for all stakeholders, including suppliers and demanders?
- Do stakeholder mindsets align for consistent work? Does any mindset need alteration?

- What is the estimated supply and demand for each option?
- Using archetype analyses, decision influencers, and choice architectures, how might you alter a tangible decision factor?

Expected results include the following:

- Tangible factors of supply and demand are identified and analyzed.
- Options are quantified within the range of acceptable economic parameters.
- A prioritized list of options is created based on step 3 analysis of tangible economic factors.
- Discussions, work, and outcomes are recorded in the project documentation.

Resources needed include the following:

- Tangible and economic profiles for all stakeholders
- Data and information on project costs, benefits, distribution levels, and competitive products and services
- Parameters on ranges of expected outcomes available for decision-making context

Worksheet

Create a worksheet to document your economic analysis of each option, including the following topics:

- Tangible inquiry and decision factors
- Data analyzed
- Learning defined and evaluated
- Priority within range of economic acceptability

Jill ensured that the team had data and information access for decision making on options' evaluation. Jill and the team prioritized the three options based on economic, tangible factors. Their criteria for this prioritization were cost and benefit factors.

> *Do you have a prioritized list of economically qualified options to consider in the next LS step?*

LS Step 4: Emotional/Mindset Analysis

LS step 4 qualifies all options identified in LS step 2 with mindset analyses of intangible factors, testing the acceptance of all stakeholders. Alignment of mindsets is the focus of step 4. Discussions might include the following:

- Who are suppliers and demanders for each option?
- What are the intangible factors of supply and demand for each option?
- What are the mindsets of these suppliers and demanders regarding each intangible factor?
- How do these mindsets align to the project mindset for each option?
- What is the gap in mindsets for the intangible factors of each option?
- Using archetype analyses, decision influencers, and choice architectures, how might you alter a mindset as an intangible decision factor?

Expected results include the following:

- Intangible factors are identified and analyzed.
- An analysis of the intangible factors for each option evaluates mindset obstacles.
- A prioritized list of options integrates step 3 and 4 prioritized options.
- The highest prioritized option is selected for implementation.
- Discussion, work, and outcomes are recorded in the project documentation.

Resources needed include the following:

- Data and information on stakeholder mindsets that impact supply and demand
- Data and information that impact supply and demand, such as association research, government research and databases, publications and relevant articles, think tank and foundation research
- Parameters on acceptable ranges of outcomes providing decision-making context

Worksheet

Create a worksheet to document your emotional/mindset analyses of each option, including the following topics:

- Intangible inquiry and decision factors
- Data and information analyzed
- Learning defined and evaluated
- Priority within range of economic acceptability

Jill continued to ensure data and information access for decision making and evaluation of options. The team reprioritized the options from step 3 to reflect another set of criteria based on mindset/emotional acceptance of stakeholders and collaborators, such as customer's ease of use, customer's perception of the value of the option, and the interest of technical builders.

Do you systematically find options to solve problems? How do you evaluate each of these options?

Being in Control With Self-Sufficiency

Building control is essential in your autonomous work. Agency enables your assertiveness and self-confidence of autonomy. Having options enables you to comprehensively evaluate all needs, project and participants, using your self-accountability of autonomy. Self-confidence and self-accountability ensure your self-sufficient control of your work, decisions, and destiny. Self-sufficiency is the ultimate goal of autonomy. It means that you rely on yourself to survive and thrive in any circumstances. LS steps 5 and 6 are focused on building your control of work and decisions.

LS Step 5: Implementation

LS step 5 focuses on defining a project plan and work to implement the workflow to build the selected option. All previous analyses are used to influence the project team plan and work. The project charter that was created in LS step 1 is useful in creating the project plan for implementation of the selected option. Discussions might include the following:

- What is the purpose and objective of the project?
- What project implementation steps need to be planned?
- Who are the stakeholders in these implementation steps?
- What is the goal of each implementation or milestone step? How will each result be measured?
- What resources are needed? Where and when are these resources available?
- What are the tools, techniques, and protocols to streamline activity, communications, and decisions?
- What is the timeline for achieving each milestone?
- How do obstacles to expected outcomes of work get resolved?
- How does review and revision of the implementation plan happen when needed?

Expected results include the following:

- Implementation steps are defined with a purpose and objective, list of stakeholders, expected results, research resources and their access, a timeline, communications protocols, and a decision-making model.
- Incremental milestone steps achieve their goals.

- Adjustments to next steps are made, as needed.
- Planned recognitions and rewards continuously motivate and align work toward the project goal, milestone goals, and final expected results.
- Project work occurs with little conflict or delay.
- Decisions are made expeditiously for achieving expected results.
- Discussions, work, and outcomes are recorded in the project documentation.

Resources needed include the following:

- LS template
- Project team template
- Communications protocol
- Decision analyses tools
- Inquiry and research tools
- Project summary templates for recording incremental project work
- Project charter
- Availability of team members

Worksheet

Create a worksheet to document project planning, including the following topics:

- Project names, description, and purpose
- People involved: collaborators, stakeholders, organization leaders, external forces, and advocate
- Expected result
- Dated current state of issue or need
- Gap to be filled
- Timeline
- Implementation steps: milestones, dates, goals, metric, and measure
- Additional stakeholders, collaborators, and contributors
- Resources needed with time estimate for each resource

- Resources available and gap to fill
- Plan to fill resource gaps
- Communication protocols
- Decision-making protocols
- Other comments

Jill defined decision-making criteria and timeframes to prompt team member decisions. She also defined parameters on what was considered new value to the new product. Jill and her team created a project plan and implemented the selected option in a timeframe that was required for delivery of the new product.

Have you defined what will indicate successful implementation of the selected option?

LS Step 6: Reflecting

LS step 6 includes considering actual versus expected outcomes for pivoting as needed, as well as identifying the benefits and impact of work completed to become aware of new opportunities. Discussions might include the following:

- What work met expected outcomes, as opposed to actual outcomes?
- What obstacles intervened to create a gap?
- How could these obstacles be removed or modified to enable the expected outcomes?
- Do the expected outcomes need to be modified?
- What impact did any and all outcomes create?
- What impact suggests current or future opportunities?

Expected results include the following:

- Reflections are focused on previous work for insights into potential improvements and new opportunities.

- Potential improvements and opportunities are analyzed to determine any new value to be created.
- Improvements and new opportunities are identified by anyone in the organization.
- A *Reflections* team manages these discussions and analyses.
- Discussions, work, and outcomes are recorded in the project documentation.

Resources needed include the following:

- Reflections template
- Data and information on previous projects and outcomes
- Contextual data and information on stakeholders, collaborators, contributors, and external forces that can or do impact current project work
- Parameters to quantify and qualify improvements and new ideas
- Decision factors, based on economic and mindset components and their implementation
- Recognition and reward process and programs
- Innovation discussions
- *Reflections* team

Worksheet

Create a worksheet to document reflection on improvements and new opportunities, including the following topics:

- Reflection and description
- Possible improvement to workflow, inputs, and outcomes
- Possible new value uncovered
- Inquiry to guide research
- Data and information needed

Jill, Jim, and the team considered each step of the project to identify where the workflow and the outcomes could be improved. They also considered any opportunities that came about during their work and the results to be achieved with each. They also made a plan for implementing any changes needed to maximize the value of their reflections.

Do you reflect on all outcomes to identify improvements or new opportunities? Do you plan to implement the changes that you identified?

Checking the Artifacts of the Project Narrative

Artifacts of your work create the narrative that will engage and encourage others to work with you and your organization. Awareness of these artifacts and their messages to colleagues, stakeholders, and the world will give you the opportunity to control them to serve you well.

Jill and Jim created credible artifacts of their autonomy with their management of the project. These artifacts included their agency by presenting ideas as well-researched and feasible to their team members. Their background research led to specific communications that described, predicted, or prescribed work to be done.

Using the Learning System gave them complete control over the work and results, specifically with the supply and demand considerations at each step. Their achievement of desired results served their company and end users very well.

Jill and Jim's work was inspirational to team members and an excellent model of how autonomous behaviors and decisions streamline communications, work, and decisions. All team members agreed that Jill and Jim modeled behaviors and decisions that were both independent and dependent on the expertise of others. Their narrative was exactly what they intended it to be.

Chapter Summary

This chapter guides an individual's autonomous mindset and skills. It establishes a process and environment to support autonomous work in the context of current work or project. The next chapter, "Building The LEGO Group's Autonomous Environment," provides an example and the results of building an autonomous environment for success.

PART 2

Building an Organizational
Environment for Autonomy

CHAPTER 4

Building The LEGO Group's Autonomous Environment

LEGOs are well known to most of the world as a unique toy. This value proposition has been revised again and again to meet customer and societal mindsets through the almost 100 years of the company's existence. The word "lego" translates into English as "play well." This word recognizes the creativity of the child within all of us and provides the opportunity for developing that creativity for unlimited innovation. This creativity lends itself to the well being of the children and adults who have been captivated by the undeniable attraction of LEGOs.

The LEGO Group (LEGOs) has evolved from a carpenter's workshop of excellently crafted woodworking into a set of plastic bricks that knows no limit to its quality and creativity. The LEGO organization has built an empire of toys that are exclusively focused on play and its developmental outcomes. Its focus on a vision of assisting child development through play, its purpose of evolving toys to be relevant in their current societal environment, and its mindset of serving workers for producing the highest quality toys have enabled it to grow and thrive for that 100 years. The leaders' intrapreneurial and entrepreneurial spirit has managed through tough times, challenges, and newly defined opportunities to become a well-known force of good will and inspiration for sharing the value of play.

The LEGO Group (lego.com) is a Danish company founded in the 1930s by Ole Kirk Christiansen. It is the world leader in the toy industry. Ole Kirk Christiansen was an idea man, always seeking new avenues to create value. His professional life began as a carpenter, building homes, barns, and anything that his neighbors in Billund, Denmark requested. His children often played with the scrapes of wood in the workshop, using their creativity to make fun toys. Ole Kirk was always taken with the notion of play, fun, and their value to children's development; thus, The LEGO name came to be.

He soon began to craft wooden toys as he so loved the idea of play and child development all rolled together. He also sold the wooden toys to supplement his business revenues. As World War II (WWII) came to an end, Ole Kirk and LEGO were challenged with the availability of supplies to make his wooden toys. And plastics were just being developed. For a period of time, the wooden toys and plastic blocks were produced simultaneously. Eventually, the company consolidated its operations and eliminated the wooden toys. The leaders became more focused on sharing the value of play with plastic blocks among multiple and diverse users. Partnerships were developed to facilitate delivery through other parts of the world. One of those successful partnerships was an agreement with *McDonald's* to provide a small sampling of LEGO bricks with each *Happy Meal*®. *McDonald's* was family-oriented and so was LEGO. Combining their products made great sense and introduced many families to the LEGO play for creative development, both for children and adults.

In the knowledge economy, The LEGO Group is venturing into its fourth generation of family leadership. Their focus for these changing times continues to be on the innovations necessary to develop the *capital of the child*. Creativity and development are their first priority. They have declared that priority as the essence of inheritance for The LEGO Group. Considering the conditions of the knowledge economy, there is no more timely focus than to contribute to workers and their autonomous well being. When workers are intentional in their development and creativity, they will sustain themselves to thrive in their own defined ways. LEGOs challenge these knowledge economy workers to find the creative child within themselves, define what they are striving to achieve, and figure out how to build it accordingly. This presents the essence of autonomy.

LEGO's leaders challenged themselves to produce what was relevant to their current and future customers, what they could offer these customers, what the future held for these customers, and how they would design their toys to accommodate the future and its systems.

These systems were identified for LEGO competitors, customers, and the social environments that always impact how people think and play. How, when, and why do people use their free play time? That insight guided LEGO's product design and development. The notion of play, as it assists the development of the child in everyone, was essential to the company's vision, purpose, and mindset.

Mindset Tendencies

Founder Ole Kirk Christiansen had natural tendencies to care for and motivate his workers from the very beginning of their careers. As he developed his carpentry business, he focused on helping workers learn from mistakes and continue their employment with him. He was never harsh in his response to their work. He observed and valued children's play as a young father and business owner. Ole Kirk would craft wooden toys mostly as a hobby in the early days but then began to sell them as part of his carpentry business. The toys became a focus of his business endeavors.

Ole Kirk's sense of decency was always demonstrated by his good relationships with his staff. When one of his apprentices finished his time learning the woodworking craft, Ole Kirk suspected that the young man had no place to go, Ole Kirk offered him a job, living quarters, and meals. Ole Kirk cared about people, their creativity, and growth.

Eras of Evolution and Development

1920s

Ole Kirk Christiansen was a young carpenter when he established a business in Billund, a small town in Denmark. He named the business *Billund Woodworking and Carpentry Shop*. The woodworking business was becoming well established with commissions for homes and barns. Most of the townspeople belonged to the *Inner Mission*, an evangelical revivalist group, with religion and God at the center of their lives. The Wall Street crash of 1929 impacted the economies of Europe and spread to Denmark as a major trading partner. Woodworking was impacted especially since there was little money for building or renovating.

1930s

As life and business became more challenging, Ole Kirk's faith carried him along. His last building project was in 1931, when he transitioned to making more wooden household items, such as stepladders, ironing boards, and a few Christmas toy cars of wood. Ole Kirk really loved making toys for children as much as he loved making buildings for adults. He was always aware of societal trends and needs. When *yoyos* became popular, he started making them.

The notion of the importance of child's play became widespread in the 1930s, and Ole Kirk tracked the current day psychologists and their rationale of connecting play, development, and learning. Ole Kirk became increasingly interested in the idea of his toys and play fostering creativity as children grew up.

In 1934, the new focus on toys suggested the need for another name. After a survey and search, LEGO was the name chosen to describe the need for good play, or to play well.

1940s

A fire disrupted the business and required a new building to be built to house the business. This new building was a testament to Ole Kirk's humane caring for his employees and family. There were options to move to another town, but Ole Kirk decided that the loyalty of the current Billund employees and family connections would be best served by rebuilding the factory in Billund. It was built to surround Ole Kirk's personal garden so that employees could have pleasant and restful work breaks.

As WWII progressed, it was important that The LEGO Group keep daily routines going to ensure continuing work in Billund. Ole Kirk was creative by cutting peat in the heath to ensure heat for the factory, supplying a gas generator to fuel cars with wood waste, and growing tobacco in his garden.

Toys, still being crafted of wood, became very much in demand as people wanted to keep their children happy and shielded from the reality of war. Sales rose from 30 to 40 percent year after year.

WWII introduced a new opportunity for Ole Kirk, which was the *peace pistol* made of wood and a metal spring mechanism for loading and shooting wooden bullets. It was a popular toy that countered the guns and violence of the war with its name. The *peace pistol* was very popular, but this was compromised by a shortage of wood in Billund and the varnish that made the black gun look so authentic. As Ole Kirk looked for substitute materials, he came across plastic, which had begun to be developed during WWII. He invested a huge sum of LEGO capital in molding machines for producing plastic *peace pistols*. Shortly thereafter, he was introduced to small toy plastic bricks from England.

LEGO pursued what looked like a great opportunity for the company but not without a diversity of opinions among family members. Ole Kirk convinced his family of the opportunity to adopt the plastic bricks by sharing his faith in the pursuit. He said that he had prayed to God about plastic bricks, and he had faith in them.

1950s

Ole Kirk's son, Godtfred, was named LEGO's Junior Managing Director. He was not as confident in plastic as he was in wood, but his father overcame his objections and won this disagreement. The plastic bricks rose to 50 percent of their revenue, including over 250 items for sale.

Godtfred was promoted to Managing Director when Ole Kirk had a disabling, but not fatal, stroke. He decided to travel to visit distributors and sellers of LEGO products and to benefit by learning about their ideas and needs. At a toy exhibit in 1951, LEGO displayed multiple toys, wooden and plastic, including their latest bestsellers from the Billund factory. Often, short-term products were popular and then declined in demand. As LEGO bricks had so many products, Godtfred decided to implement a strategy of *concentration*. This *concentration* meant focus on one product for the LEGO bricks. The *LEGO System* was born.

The *LEGO System* was not about four to six bricks being used to make a building. It was about collecting multiple sets of bricks and conceptualizing the possibilities of what one could build using any amount or arrangement of them.

The company focus would be on the plastic bricks and expanding them in multiple ways, such as collecting for birthdays, Christmas, taking apart and rebuilding in new structures, and so on. Tangential to this decision was an increasing interest in the upbringing and education of children through healthy play and good toys. Ole Kirk said, "We are undeniably living in the age of the child."

To further this thinking, Godtfred shared his vision as a four-step process for expanding the plastic LEGO bricks: step 1 was the play system for children;, step 2 was to provide a hobby for adults;, step 3 was as a tool for engineers and architects in the construction industry, and step 4 was to provide an environment and tool to change the way we think and construct our world. The LEGO Group was taking advantage of its visionary powers.

1960s

Expansion and another fire in the 1960s caused cutting back on LEGO's other products, current wooden toys, and Bilofix, which was an emerging and innovative toy. This left all focus for the plastic bricks. Multiple social considerations were explored for creating new value propositions. Also, multiple partnerships were explored to build market share. *McDonald's* was an example of a very successful partnership as *McDonald's* was known as a family restaurant offering a *Happy Meal*. When this *Happy Meal* included a small package of LEGO bricks, they made the meal even happier for family and children. Now parents and children were familiar with the value of the plastic bricks.

Expansion also included 3D design ideas for architects to envision their buildings.

1970s

A new manager, Vagn Holck Andersen, was hired to help restructure the company for expansion. Godtfred's overarching management style and energetic influence on all decisions had to change. Andersen's plan was for decentralization and delegating responsibility for decision making. Also, since there were several business locations at this point, it was essential to create a management style and structure that could facilitate decision making by the most logical people who were closest to a decision, issue, or need.

Although sales were high, the company seemed to be losing some of its spirit and energy as Godtfred aged and lost some of his energy. This spirit of venturing into unfamiliar territory seemed to decline.

It was time for Godtfred's son, Kjeld, to begin managing LEGO. He bought a Honeywell computer to be able to calculate and navigate demand forecasts and strategy. A transition from father to son had begun, and Kjeld had more progressive ideas than his father for developing new markets for children's needs across various groups.

One of these new markets was girls. Previously, LEGO toys were focused on building to satisfy boys' interests. Girls' interests brought a new need for play inside buildings. They were more focused on the area inside the buildings, such as kitchens, living rooms, and bedrooms, as opposed to the building themselves.

1980s

Creative thinking and innovation were encouraged and rewarded. A new product, *Minifigures*, lent itself to role playing, which was a new and significant element of play. LEGO play was being challenged by the game consoles that had been introduced into the markets in the 1980s. Role play was a differentiator for LEGOs and lent itself to the creative process of imagination and characterization.

LEGO continued to focus on their play systems, only implementing technology as it enhanced their main goal of providing toys for learning and development through play. This led to a partnership with the MIT Media Lab to explore the synergy between technology and children's creativity. Seymour Papert of the MIT Media Lab studied Jean Piaget's theory of how children develop through meeting challenges. Papert created a simple and intuitive programming language that children could use with a computer to guide their play with LEGO bricks.

Several LEGO brick innovations were now complete: (1) the original building system in 1955, (2) the wheel in 1962, (3) the motor in 1966, and (4) the computer programming that could build behaviors into the play with bricks.

Management had now taken a new perspective via Per Sorensen, a new manager, that all work and tasks should be considered from differing perspectives. He created the 11 paradoxes of management to guide LEGO managers in their decision making. An approach of *both/and* became more important than *either/or*. Father and son agreed to disagree on some points. The company was now so big that Godtfred no longer knew every employee. This growth resulted from Kjeld's leadership and decisions.

As LEGO was a *we* company, Kjeld sent his managers all around the world to convey this partnering narrative that would establish this sense of LEGO. Play as learning had to be understood as the LEGO brand by all of the world.

LEGO *Mindstorms* was the result of the LEGO/MIT Media Lab partnership.

1990s

Engagement and creativity seemed to be waning with LEGO. In a significant advertising campaign, LEGO *Minifigures* climbed the Berlin Wall as it toppled. Interest in LEGOs became widespread through Europe.

Kjeld became sick and had to spend time recuperating. When he finally returned, his consensus-building management model, *Compass Management*, didn't seem to be working. It required long, collaborative discussions that seemed inefficient. Kjeld realized that his communication of his vision of the future was not being understood and embraced by his managers. His vision was about the nature of the company and its attention to the inner child in everyone, as opposed to the size of the company in the future.

Digital toys were successful, but a change in management style was crippled by a lack of perceived need for change. LEGO's 3D computer designed products were introduced. The vision of meeting children needs for play in this digital age now drove the strategy of the company. LEGO *Mindstorms* and its diversity of play became a huge success.

Also, a forward-thinking approach to products introduced LEGO parks, children's clothes and shoes, watches, and so on. Partnerships with current movie producers, such as *Star Wars*, enhanced awareness and interest in LEGO toys.

Kjeld held firm in his belief that the basic bricks were the essential product of LEGO, as they fostered the creativity of children's development. The fantasy of digitization was considered an imposed feature and not the most important element for child's play to assist in creativity and development.

A new manager helped the company regain its self-confidence with a *fitness* program. This program touted the need to not only solve current problematic financial results but to prepare for the future to achieve the vision of the company. There would have to be layoffs, but employees had a great solidarity within the organization for their workplace and the family that had guided them for almost 70 years. Dissention was not wide spread.

2000s

Huge losses and a change in management set the tone for the 2000s. Kjeld would return to full responsibility for managing LEGO. He also was aware that he had to find a successor. He was so impressed with one of his junior managers that he quickly identified him as that successor. This successor, Jorgen Vig Knudstorp, recognized that he needed to consider all levels of people and their ideas. He instituted an online chat to facilitate dialog with anyone who wished to share ideas or had questions.

Knudstorp began to mingle with adult LEGO users and recognized the value in collaborating with outside users to plan for the future. This was a big change from the LEGO confidence in their own internal expertise. He also liquidated the LEGO parks and other properties to reverse their financial crises.

He changed the *fitness* management goal to one of shared vision. It included three stages that would be achieved incrementally. Employees were to make these stages part of their daily work and goals:

- To lead the industry in creating value for our customers and sales channels
- To refocus on the value we offer our customers
- To increase operational excellence

In summary, their focus was to be on innovation, not perfection.

When losses were overwhelming, there was consideration of selling The LEGO Group. A shared vision saved the company through employee commitment and creativity.

2010s

Inheritance of the business was not about money or value of the enterprise. It was about its vision of promoting the inner child in all of us and the development needed to foster creativity to become productive and contributing adults.

The LEGO Group created autonomy as a learning organization (Senge 1990), both internally and externally, to sustain itself and thrive as society and their company needs evolved.

Chapter Summary

This chapter provides an example of The LEGO Group's development for almost 100 years of growth and success. The next chapter, "Defining an Organizational Environment for Autonomy," describes the learning organization components and the process to create this environment within your organization.

CHAPTER 5

Defining an Organizational Environment for Autonomy

Community engagement is important to almost all initiatives. When a small software company decided to restructure to support worker autonomy, the effort was well-intended but unsuccessful. Several factors contributed to this failure:

- *Community confusion on expected behaviors, actions, and decisions*
- *Managers' distrust of executive management's intentions*
- *Reinforcement undefined*
- *Advocate given no authority or reinforcement tools*
- *Lack of an autonomous environment of conditions to support autonomous workers*
- *All decisions made by leaders*

Workers knew there were changes but didn't understand autonomy and how these changes impacted them or what was expected of them. They needed some help with understanding the organization's mindset and how they might match it for their own growth, as well as the benefit of the organization and its growth.

Individuals were not able to build their own autonomy within this organization. Leaders needed to focus on building worker trust and understanding of the changes and their benefits. These leaders didn't accommodate those needs, and the results of the well-intended changes were dismal. The advocate responsible for leading the change left the organization.

Change is inevitable. We often resist, but the cost of not changing may be far greater than the cost of embracing the change. Not to adapt will incur the costs of conflict resolution, redundant work, overlooked needs, missed opportunities, and potential failure. The cost of adapting to a change can be significant, but it can balance with the new value to be created, if planned well.

Managers can be very strategic in navigating the changes in the knowledge economy and its work requirements. The mindset of the organization and its leaders will define how change is managed. The knowledge economy requires that workers be autonomous in their mindsets, work, and decisions. The remoteness of work requires that workers work, behave, and make decisions that are individually determined and aligned to the organizational mindset. The organization and its leaders have to support this autonomy for workers and work to be effective.

Autonomy needs workers to be self-confident, self-accountable, and self-sufficient. Do your leaders believe that workers need continuous direction, can be totally self-reliant, or that the leaders should focus on the development and growth of the workers? How does that belief manifest itself in the organizational mindset and management?

When the narrative of your organization is that of autonomy, it is more attractive, as well as competitive, to workers seeking to associate themselves with an organization that supports their development and growth to build their careers. As workers and their careers develop and grow, so does the organization.

This chapter describes the environment that enables autonomous skills to be maximized. An organizational mindset of autonomy guides work to serve workers, leaders, and the organization for development and growth. Topics include the following:

- Defining Organizational Autonomy
- Organizational Vision and Mindset
- The Learning Environment
- The Learning Organization Model
  - Systems Thinking
  - Personal Mastery
  - Shared Vision
  - Mental Models
  - Team Learning
- Integrating Learning Organization Components

- Checking Your Artifacts and Narrative
- Chapter Summary

Defining Organizational Autonomy

Organizations want to survive and thrive. With the knowledge economy's rate of change and the availability of data and information, workers are expected to be autonomous in their agency, finding options to solve problems, and in taking control of their work.

Autonomous work is independent and dependent at the same time and is synonymous with learning. Competencies of self-confidence, self-accountability, and self-sufficiency lead the autonomous workers to establish these characteristics of agency, finding options, and taking control of decisions. Their mindsets include goals and values of autonomy, and their skills establish autonomy as they work. It is essential that autonomous workers are aware of each other's mindsets so that they can work together with minimal conflict toward the organization's vision and mindset.

The organizational mindset defines the expectations of autonomous work and establishes the organizational components that support autonomous work. This mindset defines the tenets of autonomy that support workers in their quest for working independently and dependently to complement each other's expertise and decision making. Figure 5.1 describes the organizational flow for creating an autonomous environment.

Management experts, McGregor and Ouchi, define management theories to accommodate autonomous work as it applies in various situations. McGregor's theory (Sachs 2022) includes a leader's analysis of the type of direction needed by workers. Do workers need continuous oversight and direction on their work, as indicated in *Theory X*? Or can workers determine their own work activity, behaviors, and decisions, as indicated in *Theory Y*? Ouchi (Quchi 1981) is focused on the development and growth of the worker, resulting in their excellent performance and that of the organization, as indicated in *Theory Z*.

This analysis can lead to different management based on the current scenario and the level of work. What approach or combination thereof do your workers need to be content and, also, motivated to perform at the

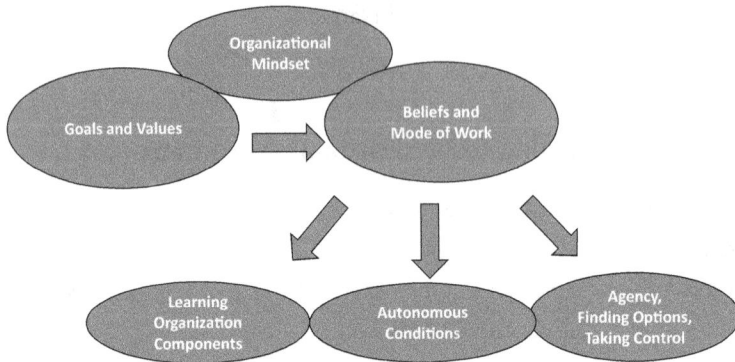

Figure 5.1 Building Organizational Autonomy

highest level possible? How is the autonomous organization accommodating these needs for contentment and motivation?

Consider workers as internal customers. The first objective in serving
these customers is to build their trust. Designing an organizational mindset that provides the direction and resources needed to be autonomous
builds worker trust. Leaders also have to establish their own trust in the
workers to work and make decisions that will lead to high organizational
performance and growth.

An autonomous environment in an organization makes sure that mindsets, both individual and organizational, guide work. This autonomous
environment is called a learning organization. Leaders and workers are
continuously seeking to understand the dynamics and mindsets involved
in collaborative work. Leaders make management choices to ensure that
autonomy and learning prevail and are reinforced continuously.

*The software company leaders were eager to share decision making
with their newly autonomous workers but didn't consider their
needs in order to make decisions. Leaders and managers were
not prepared for their employees to make decisions and didn't
really understand how they would implement or support such a
policy. They didn't consider the workers to be their customers.*

An organization in the knowledge economy is dependent on its members to develop and use their autonomy. It is responsible for setting up and
implementing the organizational mindset and structure that will enable

its members to be autonomous. These members are the most important asset of the organization, so investing in them, their work, development, and growth is essential to the organization.

> *A bad organizational structure and/or culture will kill all agency.*
> (Wargo 2024)

An organizational environment of autonomy eliminates uncertainty about what and how work will get done. Review the references to autonomy in your organizational mindset. Do they include notions of self-confidence, self-accountability, and being in control of one's work and decisions? Are autonomous behaviors recognized and rewarded as a mode of work? Are workers expected to make decisions based on learning? Are essential data and information available to support autonomous inquiry and learning for decision making? Are decisions assigned to those workers closest to an issue?

> *Company leaders would need to encourage and reward the self-confidence, self-accountability, and self-sufficiency of workers. Creating a support system for them to develop these competencies when working might include personal profiles with mindsets, development plans, and ensuring that programs and opportunities exist to accommodate their development and growth. Training on decision-making tools, techniques, and protocols would also reinforce the importance of autonomy within the organization.*

Concepts and requirements of autonomous work are described in Chapter 3. *Individual Autonomy Defined.*

Organizational Vision and Mindset

Learning is the basic requirement of autonomy. The inquiry, research, and analysis of learning fosters autonomous work. The learning organization begins with a vision and mindset that guides autonomy and learning and the environment that will support them.

Your organizational vision is your wish for the future state that you hope to create. It is implemented through your organizational mindset. This organizational mindset defines, encourages, recognizes, and rewards the elements of autonomy. Consider each mindset component and the autonomous needs within your organization:

Goals—Goals set the direction for the organization and its members.

- Consider an idealized design of the future and its needs.
- Consider the invisible capital of your organization and its members.
- Are your goals relevant and support individual and organizational growth?
- Do they include development plans, mentoring, succession planning, and reskilling training?
- Do your goals support self-confidence, self-accountability, and self-sufficiency?
- Is there a defined path for adjusting organizational goals as changes occur?
- Do your goals cover the four categories of personal, professional, community, and areas of expertise, providing multiple development paths for workers?
- Are your goals relevant to your vision of the organization?

Values—Common values within an organization create an environment where everyone works in the same mode, and decisions are made from this common perspective.

- What values do your idealized design and invisible capital identify?
- Do your values support self-confidence, self-accountability, and self-sufficiency?
- What values are relevant to your vision and goals?
- What values are relevant to your autonomy as an organization?

Beliefs—Beliefs translate your values to guide operations and work on specific projects.

- What beliefs are indicated in your idealized design and invisible capital?
- Do your beliefs recognize the biases and behavioral tendencies of your industry and domain expertise?
- Do you analyze and compare your own biases and beliefs to those of your stakeholders and collaborators?
- Do your beliefs align to your values?

Mode of work—Mode of work provides operational guidance, including metrics, decision and communication parameters, tools, techniques, and protocols, for how work is done.

- Do your idealized design and invisible capital introduce unique modes of work?
- Does your mode of work support using the seven autonomous skills?
- Does the organizational mindset and structure include these autonomous skills?
- Do you recognize and reward autonomous work?

> *What are your goals, values, beliefs, and mode of work that will build an autonomous environment to support your autonomous workers?*

> *Software company vision and mindset were not intentionally designed and shared with the organizational members. These artifacts would have paved the way for members to establish the context for building their autonomy, as enabled by the goals, values, beliefs, and mode of work described in the organization's mindset.*

This vision and mindset will guide all work within your organization, including motivation toward innovation. In an autonomous world, this work and innovation are based on continuous learning. Autonomous workers are lifelong learners. They fuel their own development and growth and that of their organizations. A learning organization model supports their efforts and outcomes.

The Learning Environment

The learning environment starts with the seven autonomous skills that all knowledge workers use to build their autonomy and success in their work. They include the following:

1. *Considers mindsets*: Knowledge workers consider the four components of mindset and their alignment to each other. Mindset considerations happen for each decision and for all stakeholders involved in a work initiative.
2. *Sets goals and pursues results*: Knowledge workers set goals as part of their work, including a hierarchy of incremental goals and results expected for each effort, including daily work.
3. *Values inquiry and learning*: Knowledge workers query on all efforts and define expected learning, including exploration of contributing mindsets.
4. *Ensures data access and uses data for decisions*: Knowledge workers use a digital nervous system (Gates 1999) to support queries with relevant data and information for decision making.
5. *Reflects on new ideas and celebrates new value*: Knowledge workers reflect on all work, initiatives, and outcomes to improve performance and to identify new ideas and opportunities to celebrate.
6. *Makes decisions*: Knowledge workers are comfortable and competent in systematic and routine decision making.
7. *Creates new value*: Knowledge workers systematically pursue improvements and opportunities to create benefits that positively impact themselves and/or their organizations.

Training programs on autonomous skills would set expectations for their use and the results expected as they enable worker autonomy. A mentoring program to help workers develop these skills as they work could be most effective.

These skills are supported by organizational conditions that enable autonomous work. They include the following:

- Organizational mindset and narrative are defined and shared, including performance and learning goals and a standardized mode of work.
- Mindset awareness and alignment are required and supported with personal profiles of data and information for individuals, stakeholders, organizations, and partners.
- A digital nervous system is available for data and information analysis and alignment of mindset, global and local trends and events, future-state potential opportunities, workflow and archetype forecasting, decision influencers, and choice architectures.
- Confidence building, inquiry, and learning orientation are facilitated through a personal profile and LS structure that guides work, teams and projects, autonomous decision making, economic and mindset evaluation, archetype workflow analysis, and future-state speculation.
- Recognition and rewards are earned by new-value initiators and contributors, sharing data on the contribution to the enterprise.
- Intrapreneuring for new ideas is supported and reinforced by a *Reflections* team.
- Management theories of X, Y, and Z are balanced situationally, as needed, using personal profiles and satisfiers to support individual and organizational growth initiatives.

The software company could develop and use these conditions to define and create the artifacts of an autonomous environment to prompt and reward autonomous work.

The Learning Organization Model

Autonomy and learning are complementary when you are working. You are actually learning to establish your autonomy. The learning organization builds the conditions and environmental framework for learning, which enables autonomy to exist. The learning organization's five components include the following:

1. *Systems thinking*: seeing the workflow and interdependencies of functions and operations throughout the organization as interdependent systems
2. *Personal mastery*: enabling and ensuring that all workers have focused on an expertise that is the focus of their individual development and growth
3. *Shared vision*: sharing the organization's vision and mindset with workers for guidance to achievement and work
4. *Mental models*: enabling and ensuring that all workers have embraced the organization's mindset when working on projects and initiatives
5. *Team learning*: ensuring and enabling metrics, tools, techniques, and protocols to guide team activities and learning as a common and continuous mode of work for all teams and their members.

When these five components operate within an organization, workers are equipped to be autonomous. They share the same mindset and, therefore, can work and learn together to thrive for their individual development and growth and that of their organization.

Systems thinking creates the context for the other four components to exist in an organization. When workers and leaders are aware of the systems that influence all work, it is easy to build the other four components to facilitate learning. Components of personal mastery, shared vision, mental models, and team learning facilitate the common mindset that enables autonomous and successful work.

These components include various systems, tools, techniques, protocols, and resources that are discussed throughout this chapter. Table 5.1 defines the relationship of autonomous skills, learning organization components, and organizational conditions.

The secret to implementing the Organizational Master Plan is the effective use of the six Ts: talk, training, time, tools, teamwork, and traceability. New ways require time to learn, time to adjust to the new procedure, and time to implement the new processes. Too many Organizational Master Plans are unsuccessful because the time required to implement them is not included in the budget. With the teamwork concept, everyone has time to stop and help someone who needs their help. This requires that everyone has an understanding of the Organizational Master Plan so they know how they interact with other organizations that are in the process of implementing it. Traceability is the key to keeping everyone informed about what they need to do to support the Organizational Master Plan and follow up on assignments to be sure they are completed on schedule. The Organizational Master Planning process applies to the public and private sectors equally as well. (Harrington and Voehl 2012)

Systems Thinking

Awareness of the organizational systems of mindset and workflows provides insight into operations and interdependencies. This awareness prepares workers to apply and integrate the components of personal mastery, shared vision, mental models, and team learning to ensure that their autonomous work and decisions are successful.

Autonomous work is independent but also dependent. The dependence on others and their knowledge or expertise is enabled by an awareness of the systems of workflow within which each works. These workflows involve multiple stakeholders and the inputs and outputs of their systems, all driven by the mindsets of the participants and how they work within these workflows. Considering who works with whom and how they collaborate is essential context for working autonomously.

Systems include the complete cycle of the mindsets, workflow steps, inputs, actions, outputs, and outcomes of work or activity. Being aware of the *whole* picture of a system allows the autonomous worker to work, behave, and make decisions from an informed perspective. Systems thinking provides the context needed to understand the systems behind workflows that can uncover stakeholders' mindsets and their tangible and intangible decision factors that guide their work and decisions.

Table 5.1 Connecting and Enabling Autonomy

Autonomous Skills	Learning Organization Components	Conditions and Environment to Enable Autonomous Skills
Ensures data access and use in decisions	Systems thinking	A digital nervous system is available for data and information analysis and alignment of mindset, global and local trends and events, future state potential opportunities, workflow and archetype forecasting, decision influencers, and choice architectures.
Reflects on new ideas and celebrates new value		Recognition and rewards are earned by new value initiators and creators, sharing data on the contribution to the enterprise.
Creates new value		Intrapreneuring for new ideas is supported and reinforced by a *Reflections* team.
Considers mindsets	Personal mastery	Mindset awareness and alignment are required and supported with personal profiles of relevant data and information for individuals, stakeholders, organizations, and partners.
		Confidence building, inquiry, and learning orientation are facilitated through a personal profile and LS structure that guides work, teams and projects, autonomous decision making, economic and mindset evaluation, archetype workflow analysis, and future state speculation.
		Recognition and rewards are earned by new value initiators and creators, sharing data on the contribution to the enterprise.

(Continued)

Table 5.1 (Continued)

Autonomous Skills	Learning Organization Components	Conditions and Environment to Enable Autonomous Skills
Considers mindset	Shared vision	Confidence building, inquiry, and learning orientation are facilitated through a personal profile and LS structure that guides work, teams and projects, autonomous decision making, economic and mindset evaluation, archetype workflow analysis, and future state speculation.
Makes decisions		
Reflects on new value and celebrates new value		Organizational mindset and narrative are defined and shared, including performance and learning goals and a standardized mode of work.
		Intrapreneuring for new ideas is supported and reinforced by a *Reflections* team.
		Recognition and rewards are earned by new value initiators and creators, sharing data on the contribution to the enterprise.
Considers mindsets	Mental models	Management theories of X, Y, and Z are balanced situationally, as needed, using personal profiles and satisfiers to support individual and organizational growth initiatives.
Makes decisions		
Reflects on new value and celebrates new value		Recognition and rewards are earned by new value initiators and creators, sharing data on the contribution to the enterprise.

(Continued)

Table 5.1 (Continued)

Autonomous Skills	Learning Organization Components	Conditions and Environment to Enable Autonomous Skills
Considers mindsets Values inquiry and learning	Team learning	Mindset awareness and alignment are required and supported with personal profiles of relevant data and information for individuals, stakeholders, organizations, and partners.
Ensures data access and uses for decisions Makes decisions		Organizational mindset and narrative are defined and shared, including performance and learning goals and a standardized mode of work.
Creates new value		A digital nervous system is available for data and information analysis and alignment of mindset, global and local trends and events, future state potential opportunities, workflow and archetype forecasting, decision influencers, and choice architectures.
		Intrapreneuring for new ideas is supported and reinforced by a *Reflections* team.

> *When you understand how you fit with others and their systems, you can structure work to fulfill their needs, as well as your own.*

Stakeholder and work systems are many, and mapping them out with inputs and outputs will help understand them for aligning work. Some systems and workflows to consider include the following:

- *Organizational mindset of autonomy*—Define your organization's mindset system, including goals, values, beliefs, and mode of work. How might a project align to the organizational mindset and its workflows?
- *Individual mindsets of autonomy*—Individual workers create personal profiles, development plans, and subsequent workflows to guide their efforts and growth. What specific characteristics or qualities do workers bring that can influence or impact the organization and this project work?
- *Stakeholders', collaborators', and partners' mindsets*—What are your stakeholders', collaborators', and partners' mindsets and workflows that will influence or impact the project work?
- *Competitors' mindsets*—What are competitors' mindsets and workflow systems and how might they influence this project?
- *External forces*—Global and local trends and events have their own systems that can impact project work. How will these systems add or detract from your project?

I refer, again, to David Brooks (2024a), NYT *columnist, who discusses the division of labor in a* New York Times *column. He suggests that division of labor, working in concert with others in a complementary and dependent way, allows the best of performance to prevail. This dependence means that all workers contribute their expertise and then rely on others to complement it with their expertise. The combined expertise becomes a proposition of "we both win." When applied to organizational life, all agree on the common platform of a desired result. They understand their own needs and the needs of their collab-*

orators to fulfill that desired result. Autonomy has made them self-confident in their own abilities, self-accountable in finding options for working with others, and self-sufficient in making decisions that will take control of the "joint" win.

Artifacts/Results of Organizational Systems Thinking

When systems thinking is prevalent in an organization, the following artifacts are demonstrated:

- Workers create workflows to see systems within work. They understand the concept of workflow inputs and outputs, cause and effect, and diverse mindsets that shape actions, behaviors, and decisions. They analyze and modify workflows, as needed, based on archetypes, decision influencers, and choice architectures for alignment and common path work.
- Workers are curious about external influences and impacts to their work and success.
- Workers have opportunities to contribute in related areas of expertise.
- A digital nervous system is available for data and information inquiry and analysis for alignment of mindset, global and local trends and events, future-state potential opportunities, workflow and archetype forecasting, decision influencers, and choice architectures.
- Systems discussions are held by the *Reflections* team on industry, markets, new technologies, partners, trends and events, global supply chains, and relevant mindsets and needs.
- Brainstorming, brain steering, and mind mapping exercises uncover systems' connections for improvements, new ideas, and opportunities.
- Opportunities and innovations are frequent due to discussions of the interconnectedness of systems.
- Workers are aware of the narrative of innovation that their systems thinking can create.

Software company leaders could build awareness of these systems and use them as guides for leaders' roles and behaviors that would encourage and reinforce worker autonomy.

Personal Mastery

Individual personal mastery strives to define achievement in four categories: personal, professional, community, and domain of expertise. Individuals define goals to establish their paths to mastery in each category and to guide their work and aspirations. The goals are based on individual mindsets, idealized design for the future, invisible capital, and current work aspirations of new challenges and experiences. The personal mastery plan is recorded in a personal profile document.

Autonomous workers and leaders recognize the link between their own growth and the growth of their organizations. They are likely to pursue their own development and growth in the context of their organizations. Often opportunities for growth are found within the systems that touch workers. Personal profiles track these connections and the opportunities they suggest. Also, workers' and leaders' personal profiles are available to all for reference when looking for help on project work.

Personal mastery work is supported with an individual development and growth plan that engages and enables the autonomous worker to build self-confidence, self-accountability, and self-sufficiency to be in control of work and decisions. Elements of personal profiles, development, and mindset; mentoring, succession planning, and reskilling; and a recognition and rewards program are suggested to create the environment for personal mastery to flourish. They are described as follows:

- *Personal profiles, development, and mindset*—Workers are encouraged to maintain a profile that includes mindset, development planning, and a record of all activity and achievements, individually and for the organization. The mindset with goals and the development plan have to be aligned to support each other. Individual mindsets will match organizational mindsets. Profile templates are provided to individuals, along with work sessions, to support their completion. Check-in sessions are also held for support in updating as work and experiences progress.

Organizational leaders use this profile to ensure that individuals are content and motivated to pursue their goals and growth. Frequent worker reviews, formal and informal, check on the progress toward individual personal mastery.

- *Mentoring, succession planning, and reskilling*—Mentoring relationships and succession planning can guide individuals' growth. Mentoring can be arranged informally or by assignment and supports individual progress toward goals and development. Succession planning makes promotion easy as there is someone identified to move into each role and function within the organization. Succession planning and mentoring can be very complementary to each other as individuals can mentor the worker who will most likely take over one's responsibilities.

In support of individuals' professional development planning, a reskilling program provides tangible service to achieving their goals and career plans. This reskilling plan will most likely be customized to a new capability or skill that an individual is seeking. It is usually an internal program with part-time work and mentoring and can involve other members who might like to gain the experience of teaching another. Reskilling programs support skill and knowledge development and can be available through formal training or through mentoring and succession planning.

- *Recognition and rewards program*—Behaviors that are rewarded continue. A program of recognition and rewards ensures the continuation of autonomous work, behaviors, and decisions. Informally, all workers can recognize autonomous work of their peers with a comment, note, or praise for a job well done. When a peer comments on an autonomous behavior, action, or decision, workers find motivation in that comment.

Formally, a rewards program with tangible prizes should be scheduled, have definite structures for awards, and have some member participation in evaluating behaviors and work to be rewarded. It is validating and trust building to workers when positive and autonomous behaviors are recognized. Workers will continue to strive to be recognized and rewarded for similar activity.

Workers are content, motivated, and satisfied. They are retained and make referrals to other talented workers. Retained workers are a benefit to the organization as their enterprise history and knowledge cannot be replaced.

Doug, the food and farm industry visionary, engaged multiple part-time workers to help him with food distribution. As the start-up grew, he hired workers to accommodate the growing partner and customer bases. Growth was so fast that workers had to figure out their work-flow and most efficient roles to keep up with demand. Doug was busy talking to new partners and setting up agreements with them to expand the business. He recognized that his workers had to make decisions and determine policy without him. At first, this was foreign to him, and he was uncertain about their decisions. After contemplating the need and benefits of the workers' autonomy, he created a program for the workers to build personal profiles and plans for the development and growth that would ensure their self-confidence, self-accountability, and self-sufficiency for running the business, that is, to develop their personal mastery.

Artifacts/Results of Personal Mastery Expected

Personal mastery is demonstrated as follows:

- Each organizational member has a personal profile that includes goals, values, beliefs, mode of work, a development plan, and a description of the narrative intended.
- Workers are content, motivated, and satisfied, demonstrating continuous inquiry, research, learning, and frequent

intrapreneurial activity. They are retained and make job referrals to other talented workers.

- Individual profiles are updated frequently as they evolve with the shared vision and mental models of the organization. Workers are known for their strengths, interests, collaborative work habits, and achievements.
- Mindset awareness and alignment are required and supported with relevant data and information on individuals, stakeholders, organizations, and partners.
- Recognition and rewards are earned for new value creation.
- Workers are aware of the narrative that the artifacts of their personal mastery can create.

Software company workers needed personal plans for their development and growth. Leaders needed to understand these plans, support them, and ensure opportunities to facilitate their implementation. Workers had quietly quitted based on their lack of context to be autonomous.

Shared Vision

The organization's vision is a desired future state that the founders strive to create. Organizations have mindsets that guide workers and work in the common direction of that vision.

The organization's shared vision and mindset should be available for all workers to reference, as needed. This documentation can also include examples of projects, behaviors, and decisions that demonstrate an organization's environment and history. An organization's vision can also include an environment and mode of work that builds worker autonomy and development. This vision and environment would contribute greatly to the organization's narrative as a good place to work.

Time should be allocated for workers to ponder, apply, and record the shared vision and mindset within their work. It might be scheduled into a team or project agenda as part of preparation and planning time.

An organization's vision and mindset are defined based on its purpose, including its idealized design and invisible capital. Idealized design takes the future into account when creating the vision, mindset, and goals for the organization. An organization's invisible capital includes all of the strengths, interest, and experiences of everyone in the organization.

> *Does your organizational mindset utilize its idealized design and invisible capital to its best advantage?*

In the context of its idealized design and invisible capital, this mindset must support autonomous work. This support includes a mindset of goals, values, beliefs, and mode of work that expect and support workers' self-confidence, self-accountability, and self-sufficiency of autonomy

> *Consider recent actions, decisions, and their results. Consider the autonomy of that work and result. Was that autonomy supported?*

Sharing vision is essential to bring all workers and leaders to the same understanding of organizational direction. A shared vision is parallel to individual personal mastery as both provide direction for work to be done. When this vision is shared, it will frame all organizational work and build a sense of trust between leaders and workers. Trust, advocacy, clarity on leader and worker roles, budget sharing, and a *Reflections* team are all vehicles for sharing vision to support autonomy. They are described as follows:

- **Trust:** Trust is a critical factor in creating an environment for autonomy. Defining and using the organizational vision and mindset build the foundation for trust within the organization. When all work, activities, and decisions are made from the same platform, all workers and leaders know what to expect and how to guide their work. Workers trust leaders to deliver on the organizational mindset, and leaders trust workers to autonomously deliver high-quality and results-oriented work that is aligned to that mindset.

Trust also greatly facilitates remote work as is often required in the knowledge economy. This trust is the most important asset an organization can build as it ensures commitment to its workers and toward the leaders in the organization, assuming the development and growth of all. Trust builds high organizational performance. Worker's autonomous skills are not possible without a trusting environment that supports them. Figure 5.2 describes the impact of shared vision on trust and autonomy.

> *Have your leaders built trust with their behaviors, activities, and decisions? Do leaders' expectations meet those of the workers? How do workers build leaders' trust in their work? Both groups are beholden to the other to build a trusting environment for achieving the goals of the organization and the development of the workers and the organinzation.*

When asked if he had any conflicts among workers, Doug, a food and farm innovator, thought for what seemed to be an extensive reflection and said that he couldn't think of any problems with his workers. He had built so much trust with shared vision and autonomous responsibility that workers were content and motivated to deliver on that vision and be a part of a developing community.

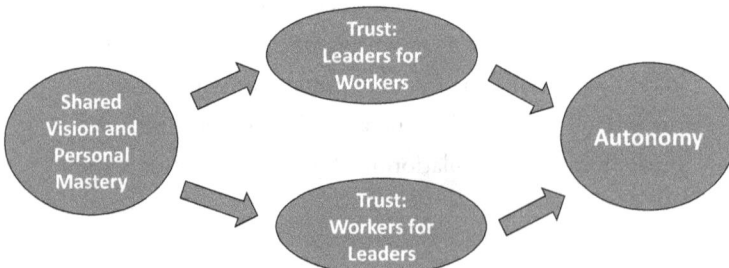

Figure 5.2 Shared Vision, Personal Mastery, and Trust

- *Advocacy:* Advocacy is a support system for aligning behaviors, actions, and decisions toward the shared vision of the organization. Direction, beliefs, and mode of work are defined in the shared vision and mindset of the organization. However important this information might be, it is only useful when it is actually applied to daily work. The shared vision and mindset of the organization should be prevalent in all work and decisions. Continuous advocating is an ongoing necessity so that the shared vision is kept top of mind for all.

Building advocacy for the shared vision is critical to its use. This advocacy can be done project by project, functional group, or on an individual basis. It might be done through a recognition and rewards program. Advocates are the experts on the shared vision and mindset and how they are integrated into the work of the organization. An advocacy role should be considered one of service to the workers and the organization.

> *How do you advocate for the shared vision and mindset in your organization?*

- *Leader and worker roles:* Leader and worker roles in an autonomous organization are often similar. Autonomous workers are leaders of their work using their agency, finding options, and control of work and decisions. However, there may be levels of decisions that need consultation with an organizational leader when clarification or a deviation from the mindset is needed. A leader's decision might be needed when a project requires a higher level of funding than is noted in the organization's mode of work.
- *Budget sharing:* Relevant budget sharing is helpful to autonomous workers as another contextual dimension in planning work. Cost and spending parameters are essential to those who are making decisions on creating new value through intrapreneurial projects. Also, budget sharing can bring further context when considering the overall value

that work brings to the organization. Budget sharing builds credibility and trust between workers and leaders. Why some expenditures can happen and others cannot is better understood.

Balancing costs, benefits, and impact of work builds worker understanding and relevant decisions to pursue new work. A Benefits/Impact Summary is a tool that gives context for expenditures and the benefits gained. Figure 5.3 provides context and rationale for budget sharing.

Software company leaders couldn't fathom sharing budget information with workers. Speculation on how workers would use the budget information was not of a trusting nature.

Also important is the path for requesting, quantifying, and qualifying new budget expenditures. Workers should understand the process for making requests and securing resources for underfunded or new work.

- **Reflections team**: A formal team, *Reflections*, is formed to conduct regular reflection sessions on project wins and losses. This team will review multiple aspects of organizational work

Benefit/Impact	Calculation	Sample Organization Details
Time Savings	Hours of work eliminated: $/hour	Combined workflows
Cost Savings	Fees for materials and services eliminated	Replaced text editing with a new text application
Revenue Generated	New product or service delivery	Added new automated customer service related to data entry
New Business Concepts	$ from new products, services, customers minus costs	Added new ancillary product to accompany main product, increasing distribution to a new market
New Business Pipeline	Potential $ from new customers	Added new product use for a new customer base
Supporting Endeavors	Potential $ from supporting initiatives minus costs	Added email service to phone services
Infrastructure Development	$ generated from streamlining or enhancing delivery minus costs	Created a new quality team to replace quality work within each operational workflow

Figure 5.3 Benefits/Impact Summary

and outcomes. It will also hold forward-thinking discussions on the state of world events and trends, industry changes, and customer and competitor activities to identify new opportunities.

These sessions may be open to any worker who wishes to participate. As sessions use the organizational vision and mindset as context, they provide a valuable opportunity to reflect on and reinforce the autonomous thinking and work that has contributed to the shared vision.

Artifacts/Results of Shared Vision

Shared vision demonstrates the following:

- A known advocate is supportive of all autonomous work and workers.
- Workers have aligned their individual mindsets to support the organization, its mindset, and its endeavors.
- Organizational vision, mindset, and narrative are defined and shared, including performance and learning goals and a standardized mode of work.
- Personal mastery, inquiry, and learning focus teams, projects, and autonomous decision making toward the shared vision of the organization.
- Workers are aware of the narrative that the artifacts of their shared vision can create.

The software company leaders should create a vision and an organizational mindset that will create trust, understanding of direction, and support for achievement. Review and refinement of this vision and mindset should be a periodic event and include the thoughts of workers and their invisible capital of strengths, interests, experiences, and network of associates and industry knowledge.

Mental Models

Mental models are specific to an organization, its vision, and its mindset. Consider mental models as the common platform of values, beliefs, and mode of work that guide all work and decisions. These mental models give context for how work will be done, leading to little conflict, ease of decision making, and a consistent focus on a common goal. Work and decisions need to align and support these values, beliefs, and mode of work for best individual productivity and performance of the organization. When working with colleagues, stakeholders, and partners, it is important that all agree on the same mental models to frame work and decisions in a consistent manner.

Behaviors result from the mental models of organizational members, stakeholders, and partners. These models define expected behaviors that facilitate autonomous work or not.

Examples of mental models that build autonomy include a service orientation; supply and demand factors; inquiry and learning; decisions, results, and persistence; social engagement, behavioral tendencies or bias awareness; reinforcing autonomy; a management system; and retaining workers and customers. They are described as follows:

- *Service orientation*—A service orientation will guide workers to consider how their contributions provide service to others. Service gives workers a broader perspective when working as opposed to focus on meeting an individual's own goal. Their individual mindsets are important for guiding their work but cannot be the only perspective to consider. Service recognizes and accommodates another's mindset and beliefs or biases. Perhaps mental model discussions can include the service orientation as a key topic.
- *Supply and demand decision factors*—Supply and demand decision factors, tangible and intangible, are rooted in workers' mindsets, including their beliefs/biases and resulting behavioral tendencies. Understanding these behaviors in the context of supply and demand decision factors gives clarity on their decisions. These factors are based on mental models

of values, beliefs, and mode of work. Consider the mental models of your colleagues when working together and making decisions. Building alignment of these models will build agreement. Supply and demand thinking is a mental model to structure all work within the organization.

The LS steps are designed to uncover these variables so that supply and demand can be balanced to meet each other. This meeting of supply and demand creates a positive direction toward achieving the common goal.

The concept of supply and demand was absent in all work within the software company culture. Leaders and workers did not consider the needs of their collaborators and how they might fulfill those needs along with their own needs. Leaders did not consider the workers as their suppliers, and workers didn't consider themselves demanders with their own needs, tangible and intangible.

The organization did not develop a mental model to support the new culture. The leaders were oblivious to the needs of workers to be able to implement the new culture.

Changes to supply and demand decision factors can be facilitated with archetype workflow analyses, decision influencers, choice architectures, or simply changing the goal of the project.

How do you usually manage gaps and obstacles?

Sometimes goals need to be changed to accommodate suppliers and demanders. Through the analyses of demanders' and suppliers' mental models, a project goal may turn out to be not feasible, no longer important, or not really urgent. This is valid insight provided by the mindsets of the workers involved. The goal can be changed to be acceptable to the supplier and the demander.

- *Inquiry and learning*—Inquiry and learning are essential to an autonomous environment. It is important at every step in the LS that guides autonomous work. Inquiry and learning support an openness to alternative options as opposed to making status quo decisions. They define options for a solution to a problem or new need. Asking the right questions and being open to other questions that arise are important aspects of being autonomous. Inquiry into how and what others think is especially important for working with them successfully. Consider the mental models that influence their decisions for insights into the tangible and intangible decision factors that impact supply and demand matches.

> *How does your organization consistently reinforce inquiry and learning?*

- *Making decisions, getting to a result, persistence*—A mental model of autonomy has a focus on making decisions, getting to a result, and persisting in work to pursue a goal. Expecting and monitoring these worker actions can recognize and reward them to reinforce their consistent practice. Regular recognition motivates workers to use these skills, as well. The outcomes of these skills can be observed and rewarded.
- *Social engagement*—Building social experiences motivates workers' familiarity with each other and results in establishing relationships. Social experiences (Zynga 2014) can include relaxing time, physical social spaces, and collaborative *think tank* programs that enhance relationships and innovative exploration. These relationships improve productivity, contentment, and motivation of workers. Workers who socialize with each other work better together than when they work with unfamiliar colleagues. A mental model of familiarity is conducive to awareness, alignment, and collaboration among workers, as well as among stakeholders and partners.

Also, encouraging workers to organize and lead various social experiences brings trust, engagement, and recognition to individuals while building awareness of their interests and strengths.

- *Behavioral tendencies or bias awareness*—Behavioral tendencies (Ariely 2009) are the result of individual beliefs/biases or mental models. They can be considered when exploring stakeholders', colleagues', and partners' mindsets to predict their behaviors and decisions.

This analysis gives the opportunity to accommodate or modify those beliefs/biases for a match to the project mindset. It is also possible that a diverse belief or bias could add value to the project mindset. The mental model practice of archetype workflow analyses, decision influencers, and choice architectures to modify beliefs or biases is a path to alignment for a match.

How can certain behaviors impact your work and decisions?

- *Possibilities for managing systems*—A mental model for selecting various management theories is supportive of an autonomous environment. A management theory can vary depending on needs of differing situations within the work of various projects. When systems integrate and work with each other, leaders can take control by managing most effectively to build alignment within those systems.

These management theories, as previously described, give leadersoptions for taking control as needed by the project. Onemanagement theory assuredly doesn't cover all needs of autonomouswork, so leaders can vary their management approaches asapplicable to specific worker and project needs.

Software company leaders used only theory X management techniques. Autonomy requires a balance of all three management theories, X, Y, and Z. When a new worker needs to explore the systems that impact work, it could be best to provide theory X direction. When that same worker finds a discrepancy in that direction, theory Y could be useful since a worker evaluation and adjustment is appropriate. The autonomous worker can consider options for that adjustment. Finally, when that worker is feeling dissatisfied with work assignments, it could be time for the leader to use theory Z to motivate the worker to engage in expanded organizational work to find an opportunity for development.

These theories are relevant to building individual and organizationalautonomy. Selective and situational management contributes tothe mental model of taking control.

- ***Reinforcing autonomy***—A mental model of autonomy can be established and maintained by building an awareness of the five learning organization components for autonomy and the three characteristics of individual autonomy. This context sets the expectations of working autonomously, sets a definition of autonomy, and encourages autonomy in collaboration. The mental model of autonomy should result in members taking control of their own development and growth as it contributes to organizational growth.

Autonomy is about agency, options, and control. The mental model of autonomy builds understanding of what these characteristics and seven autonomous skills look like when used within the organization. These skills are supported with the seven conditions of organizational autonomy. All aspects of autonomy are also celebrated with recognition and rewards.

- ***Retaining workers and customers***—When there is a mental model for building retention, everyone is working with that in mind. Analysis of needs is an ongoing endeavor in the attempt to retain workers and customers. This mental model results from other mental models that guide effective work and relationships that will foster retention. Retaining workers and customers is often based on a revisit to a common goal that ties people and their efforts together.

Artifacts/Results of Mental Models

Mental models demonstrate the following:

- Workers share the same goals, values, beliefs/biases, and mode of work regarding the work that they do in the context of the organization and its vision and mindset.
- Organizational values are apparent to the outside world due to worker behaviors and decisions on work and individual projects.
- Diverse management theories are prevalent as needed by various scenarios.
- The organization is understood to be a contributor to society as indicated in its vision, mindset, and work.
- The organization and leaders are focused on worker development and growth, as well as organizational growth.
- Autonomous skills are expected, observable, and practiced routinely.
- Mindset awareness and alignment are required and supported with personal profiles of relevant data and information regarding individuals, stakeholders, organizations, and partners.
- Workers are aware of the narrative that the artifacts of their mental models can create.

All software company workers need to have the same expectations, or mental models, for how to work, decisions to be made, and results to be achieved. If a worker is not aware of an expected mode of work, the mental model will not expedite work. Decisions will be made in a random fashion.

Team Learning

Often twenty-first century work is done in a team structure and each member of the team has autonomous responsibilities as specific roles require. Collaboration is always needed for agreement, expertise, and availability of resources. In all cases, collaboration is learning-oriented and predominant in an autonomous mode of work. Workers use their agency to seek options for solutions and to take control of the project work, as relevant to their areas of expertise. Team learning is essential to development and growth.

Teams create a framework to enable team work, inquiry, research, analysis, and learning to ensure consistent, continuous progress. This framework consists of the other learning organization components; metrics; inquiry, research, and analyses using a digital nervous system of data and information; tools for configuring work and analyses; techniques and protocols to guide work and make decisions; a LS; and reflection, recognition, and rewards of autonomous work and results. They are described as follows:

- *Learning organization components*—The learning organization components provide preparation and background for team learning. They frame the mindset of all workers.

  Systems thinking provides insights into collaborators, stakeholders, and partners with all of their unique systems that guide their workflow of inputs and outputs. Teams will build awareness of these systems once they have identified all stakeholders, partners, and contributors in the team's work. The influence and impact of these systems will be considered when defining the team's workflow so that gaps, obstacles, and new opportunities are uncovered.

  Personal mastery ensures that workers have expertise to enable their decision making. Personal contributions to team work are driven by their mastery and the development path by which team members are evolving skills and new mastery.

  Shared vision ensures that all workers on the team have the same context of vision and mindset of the organization. This common context ensures that work and decisions are made toward that common direction.

Mental models ensure that all workers on the team have the same values, beliefs/biases, and mode of work when working and making decisions. Assumptions about what and how work is done align when workers have the same mental model from which to work. This common frame of mental models expedites work and decisions.

- *Metrics*—Metrics give context and a goal for all work.
  This end in mind gives context and direction on what will determine success of each effort or activity. These metrics are measured in relevant ways that are easily observed and can be learning-oriented or performance-oriented. Learning goals will target the inquiry and research needed to reach a performance goal. Learning goals are often tied to incremental steps in the team's workplan toward its project goal, which is usually a performance goal.

- ***Inquiry, research, and analyses using a digital nervous system***—Team learning is driven by relevant inquiry, research, and analyses of decision factors. These practices are supported by tools that shape inquiry and research to allow relevant analyses and findings. Inquiry and research are supported by a digital nervous system of data and information relevant to your organization and its goals, as well as external forces, trends, and events. Inquiry can create a description of a situation, a prediction of the outcomes of that situation, or a prescription of a path to solve the situation.
  Using the digital nervous system allows data-driven decisions. Autonomy is based on learning, and learning is based on availability and accessibility of data and information. A digital nervous system might include the following:

- Industry data and information
- Stakeholder and member profiles
- Organizational vision and mindset
- Previous project stories
- Competitor profiles
- Current trends and events
- Association and Foundation research reports
- Economic statistics from government research and agencies
- Any other data and information sources that are related to current work domains

A nervous system supports all activity of an entity and is critical to its sustainability. In the knowledge economy, this nervous system can be digital, making its contents easily available to all knowledge workers.

- *Tools for configuring work and analyses*—A set of tools that can be standardized within the organization facilitates work and its outcomes, as all workers are using the same paths to get to these outcomes. The tools of autonomy can be varied and depend on the industry, community, and worker skills of the organization. They provide structures to guide inquiry, research, and analyses for ensuring team learning, including *brainstorming, brain steering, mind mapping, five whys, Bloom's Taxonomy, archetype workflow analyses* with decision influencers and choice architectures, the LS steps, and individual profiles. Tools can be further useful to support techniques and protocols for consistency and expediency.

- *Techniques and protocols to guide work and make decisions*—Techniques are structures for implementing all team learning. They support autonomous work and decision making. Protocols are standardized approaches for using techniques that help expedite and streamline flow of work and outcomes. Techniques and protocols are enablers that set work expectations and are usually available in template formats for easy access and use. Table 5.2 lists some techniques and protocols that are useful to team learning.

- *LS:* A system for inquiry and learning is an incremental structure for ensuring that work systematically achieves

Table 5.2 Techniques and Protocols

Technique	Standardized Protocol
Project charters	Define topics to be shared with teams for developing a common mindset and platform to guide work, including a timeline for expected progress of team work, project purpose, workflow implementation, timeframe expected, and a range for desired results of a project.
Communication expectations of purpose, frequency, and formats	Define stages, styles, and formats of communication to provide frameworks for incremental and timely presentation, audience analysis, and streamlining of messaging.
Decision parameters	Determine who makes decisions, along with a range of acceptable decisions.
Decision analyses	Analyze supply and demand tangible and intangible decision factors for streamlining decision making.
Archetype analyses, decision influencers, and choice architectures	Compare gaps, obstacles, or opportunities to archetype workflows with results; identify actions for reaching or changing an action or decision.
Budgeting parameters	Define amounts of spending allowed, who can make budgeting requests, and who can change budgeting amounts.
Project summary document	Monitor and record all project activity, decisions, and outcomes for reflective reference and learning.

project goals. Project teams use the LS as a common approach to keeping project work on track, monitoring, and building progress toward a desired result.

The LS consists of six steps, as previously described. These steps are each guided by a set of questions that are answered with relevant data and information collection, analyses, and learning. This inquiry should lead to a match of supply and demand levels on work and decisions. The questions reflect the seven autonomous skills that will ensure good decision making. The steps are detailed in Chapter 3. *Building Individual Autonomy.*

- *Reflection, recognition, and rewards*—Reflecting on previous work and its outcomes is integrated into all team and individual work. Discussions of actual outcomes uncover gaps, obstacles, overlaps, and new opportunities and are a critical part of team learning. A *Reflections* team routinely meets to hold discussions on previous team work and learning. Analyses can create a path forward to resolve these outcomes, as needed.

Since the team learning component defines how work actually gets done, it is a good place for reflecting on the other four components of the learning organization environment and their contributions to autonomy. Are systems thinking, personal mastery, shared vision, and mental models contributing as needed to worker and organizational autonomy? Are updates or changes needed to any of the other components of the learning organization to continue to maintain workers' autonomy, team learning, and expected work results?

Autonomous work is recognized and often rewarded. Work is reviewed in the *Reflections* team discussion so that recognition and rewards can reinforce its autonomous nature. Also, recognition can be made by any worker toward another worker. Rewards are usually more formal with documented criteria and a scheduled routine for awarding them.

Recognition and rewards are the essential reinforcement for motivating autonomous work in a learning organization. Open dialog brings attention to recognition and reward. Workers' autonomous perspectives will continuously introduce new and relevant ideas to be recognized and rewarded. The knowledge economy is always evolving, as will new work through the autonomous innovation of workers and organizations.

Does learning always drive your work and pursuits?

The learning organization model creates the autonomous environment that supports worker's autonomous thinking.

Artifacts/Results of Team Learning Expected

Team learning demonstrates the following:

- Learning organization components are routinely revisited to ensure their value to facilitating organizational autonomous work.
- Organizational mindset is defined and shared with all members.
- Mindset awareness is a first priority in all team work.
- Individuals and teams reach their goals in the timeframes planned. They make adjustments as they work based on continuous analyses of work results and mindsets that are guiding that work.
- There are metrics, tools, techniques, and protocols that facilitate the work and expedite decision making.
- Conflicts are minimal and are easily resolved.
- Supply and demand context guides all decision making and agreement.
- Considerations of new opportunities are discussed and can be suggested by any team member.
- A digital nervous system is available for data and information analyses of mindsets, global and local trends and events, future-state potential opportunities, workflow and archetype forecasting, decision influencers, and choice architectures.
- An LS guides all work in a consistent manner.
- Recognition and rewards are earned by new value creators/ contributors, and information is shared on the contribution to the enterprise.
- Teams are perceived as leaders in the learning of the organization, as learning is established as the most important work.
- Workers are aware of the narrative that the artifacts of their team learning can create.

Team learning is probably the most powerful component of the learning organization as it creates and refines goals and work with continuous feedback. Software company leaders could benefit from this feedback on the needs of the workers to be autonomous. Are work and decisions going as planned? What changes might help reinforce autonomy and reach intended results more consistently?

Integrating Learning Organization Components

The learning organization components are complementary to each other as they impact and influence each other as part of a system. Understanding these relationships will bring a level of clarity to their workflow and how they may be in support of each other or not. If your systems understanding only extends to the personal mastery of your own skills and work, your organization will not reap the benefits of the shared vision and mental model of others to assist in your work. Your work will not be autonomous because your perspective is independent but not dependent on others for expertise or resources. Figure 5.4 depicts the integration of flow between and among learning organization components.

Workers will embrace all the components of the learning organization to build their autonomy. Learning organization components may be defined but not readily available to workers. Leaders must ensure that all the aspects of the learning organization components are within members' awareness and accessibility for applying to their autonomous work. It is not enough that these components are defined. Leaders' work is about ensuring that the learning organization components are easily applied to all work.

What is your feedback process for monitoring members' use of the learning components?

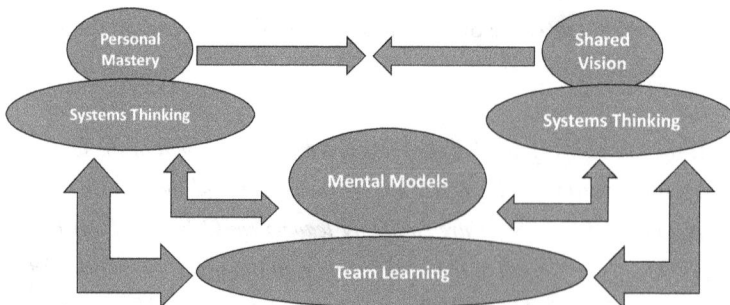

Figure 5.4 Integrating Learning Organization Components

Checking Your Artifacts and Narrative

The artifacts listed above for each learning organization component will contribute to your narrative. Reviewing your narrative as it exists with your workers, customers, collaborators, stakeholders, and partners will give good insights into the credibility of those artifacts. It is important to know the impact of these artifacts so that you can modify them to deliver the narrative you wish to have. How do these groups think of you and your organization?

Chapter Summary

This chapter describes what organizational leaders need to consider when building an autonomous environment to meet the needs of their autonomous workers. The next chapter, "Building an Organizational Environment for Autonomy," describes the process to develop a learning organization to create the autonomous environment that will support knowledge workers' autonomous work in an organization.

CHAPTER 6

Building an Organizational Environment for Autonomy

LEGO founder, Ole Kirk Christiansen, had natural tendencies for development and growth. He was a wood worker by trade and was always looking at the world around him for new opportunities. Ole Kirk also saw obstacles as opportunities. His thinking was big, always, and this led to his instincts to create a learning organization to implement his ideas. Learning was the key to turning his ideas into success. His woodworking business evolved into a toy business with worldwide acclaim. He created an environment to take advantage of his ideas and the workers who would implement them.

An autonomous environment is all about learning, learning about yourself, others, and how to manage the challenges of the twenty-first century knowledge economy. Being a lifelong and expert learner makes you autonomous. Building a learning organization prepares and supports workers to develop the autonomy they need to work in this knowledge economy.

When the narrative of your organization is that of learning and autonomy, it is more attractive, as well as competitive, to workers seeking to associate themselves with an organization that supports their development and growth to build their careers. As workers and their careers develop and grow, so does the organization. Figure 6.1 describes how to establish autonomy in your organization.

This chapter describes the environment that enables autonomous skills to be maximized. The organizational mindset and learning structures create that environment to guide work in a manner that

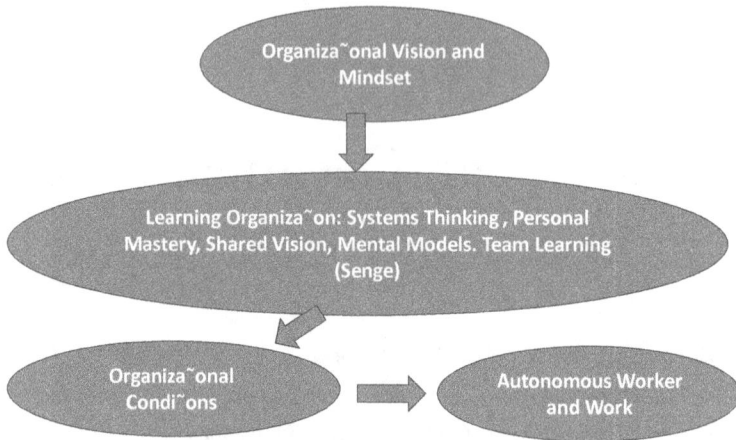

Figure 6.1 Organizational utonomy

propels workers, leaders, and the organization to thrive. Topics include the following:

- The Learning Environment for Autonomy
- Preparing Organizational Learning Tthrough a Project
- Building an Organizational Mindset for Learning
- Implementing the Five Organizational Learning Components and Programs
- Checking the Artifacts of the Project Narrative
- Chapter Summary

The Learning Environment for Autonomy

An autonomous environment in an organization makes sure that mindsets, both individual and organizational, guide work. An organization is dependent on its members to develop and use their individual autonomy, which is defined in their mindsets and enabled by an autonomous environment. This autonomous environment is called a learning organization. It sets up and implements an organizational mindset and structure that will enable its members to be autonomous. Members are the most important asset of the organization, so investing in an environment to support them and their work is essential to an

Table 6.1 *Learning Organization Components and Conditions*

Learning Organization Components	Conditions Created for Learning
Systems thinking—seeing workflow and interdependencies of functions and operations throughout the organization as systems.	A digital nervous system is available for data and information analysis and alignment of mindset, global and local trends and events, future state potential opportunities, workflow and archetype forecasting, decision influencers, and choice architectures.
	Recognition and rewards are earned by new value creators/contributors, sharing data on the contribution to the enterprise. Intrapreneuring for new ideas is supported and reinforced by a *Reflections* team.
	Intrapreneuring for new ideas is supported and reinforced by a *Reflections* team.
Personal mastery—enabling and ensuring that all workers have mastered an expertise that is the focus of their individual development and growth.	Mindset awareness and alignment are required and supported with personal profiles of relevant data and information for individuals, stakeholders, organizations, and partners.
	Confidence building, inquiry, and learning orientation are provided through a personal profile and LS structure that guides work, teams and projects, autonomous decision making, economic and mindset evaluation, archetype workflow analysis, and future state speculation.
	Recognition and rewards are earned by new value creators/contributors, sharing data on the contribution to the enterprise.
Shared vision—sharing the organization's vision and mindset with workers for guidance to achievement and work.	Confidence building, inquiry, and learning orientation are provided through a personal profile and learning system structure that guides work, teams and projects, autonomous decision making, economic and mindset evaluation, archetype workflow analysis, and future state speculation.
	Organizational mindset and narrative are defined and shared, including performance and learning goals and a standardized mode of work.

(Continued)

Table 6.1 (Continued)

Learning Organization Components	Conditions Created for Learning
	Intrapreneuring for new ideas is supported and reinforced by a *Reflections* team.
	Recognition and rewards are earned by new value creators/contributors, sharing data on the contribution to the enterprise.
	Intrapreneuring for new ideas is supported and reinforced by a *Reflections* team.
Mental models—enabling and ensuring that all workers have embraced the organization's mindset when working on projects and initiatives.	Management theories of X, Y, and Z are balanced situationally, as needed, for contentment and motivation to support individual and organizational growth initiatives.
	Recognition and rewards are earned by new value creators/contributors, sharing data on the contribution to the enterprise.
Team learning—enabling and ensuring metrics, tools, techniques, and protocols to guide team activities and learning as a common and continuous mode of work for all teams and their members.	Mindset awareness and alignment are required and supported with personal profiles of relevant data and information for individuals, stakeholders, organizations, and partners.
	Organizational mindset and narrative are defined and shared, including performance and learning goals and a standardized mode of work.
	A digital nervous system is available for data and information analysis and alignment of mindset, global and local trends and events, future state potential opportunities, workflow and archetype forecasting, decision influencers, and choice architectures.
	Intrapreneuring for new ideas is supported and reinforced by a *Reflections* team.

organization. An organizational environment of autonomy eliminates the uncertainty of what work and how work will get done.

A bad organizational structure and/or culture will kill all autonomy. (Wargo 2024)

A learning organization has five components (Senge 1990), including systems thinking, personal mastery, shared vision, mental models, and team learning. These components establish the environment in which all workers are expected to be autonomous with their individual learning paths and efforts. They create the environmental conditions that enable these expectations of autonomy to be met. Table 6.1 connects the learning organization to the conditions needed to be autonomous.

Preparing Organizational Learning through a Project

Creating the learning organization with the context of a project makes the endeavor more tangible, both to leaders and workers in the organization. This project can define the learning organization components, as needed, to build autonomy within your specific organization. Consider the following planning for your project:

- Project purpose and desired result include an idealized design and consideration of invisible capital. What is the need of this project and what benefit will it yield?
- Define the project mindset of goals, values, beliefs, and mode of work that will lead to the desired result you are seeking. Align these mindset components to support each other.
- Consider how autonomous work will be needed for this project.
- Consider the learning organization components and how they need to be shaped to support the autonomous work on this project. Refer to the project mindset for ideas on autonomous needs.

Building an Organizational Mindset for Learning

An organizational mindset sets the foundation and platform for an autonomous organization. Once defined, this foundation will guide the development of the learning components of systems thinking, personal mastery, shared vision, mental models, and team learning.

Your organizational mindset should include notions of self-confidence for agency, self-accountability for finding options, and self-sufficiency for being in control of one's work and decisions. Are autonomous behaviors recognized and rewarded in that mindset? Is learning through inquiry, research, and analysis prevalent in all decision making? This organizational mindset encourages, recognizes, and rewards the elements of autonomy.

Worksheet

Consider and document each mindset component and the autonomous needs within your organization and project:

Goals—Goals set the direction for the organization and its members. Consider an idealized design and the invisible capital within your organization.

Values—Common values within an organization create an environment where everyone works in the same mode, and decisions are made from this common ground.

Beliefs—Beliefs translate your values to guide operations and work on specific projects.

Mode of work—Mode of work provides operational guidance, including metrics, decision and communication parameters, tools, techniques, and protocols, for how work is done.

The LEGO Group founder set the mindset of the company at its earliest stage of development. Ole Kirk was sensitive to the needs of people, their families, and their need to develop and grow. He was continuously focused on providing for families, workers, and the customers that the company sought to serve. He was motivated to ensure that the company and its products were current and competitive so that the company could survive and thrive. The goal was not about money or company size, it was about the well-being of children and adults through the products that would develop their creativity.

> *What are your goals, values, beliefs, and mode of work that will build an autonomous environment to support your autonomous workers?*

Now you are ready to define and build the learning organization components that will support autonomous work to deliver on your goals, values, beliefs, and mode of work.

Implementing the Five Organizational Learning Components and Programs

Based on your organizational mindset and current project, consider the five components of the learning organization and how they should be structured to build the environment needed to support your autonomous knowledge workers.

The software company culture could have been easily created with a learning organization environment. Systems thinking, personal mastery, shared vision, mental models, and team learning provide the context, background, and skills needed to build, support, and sustain the autonomous environment to facilitate learning and the use of autonomy.

A learning organization has five components: systems thinking, personal mastery, shared vision, mental models, and team learning. These components are created and facilitated by various systems, tools, techniques, protocols, and resources that are discussed throughout this chapter.

Systems Thinking

Autonomous work is independent but also dependent. The dependence on others and their knowledge and expertise is enabled by an awareness of the systems of workflow within which they work. These workflows involve multiple stakeholders and the inputs and outputs of their systems, all driven by the mindsets of the participants and how they work within these workflows. Considering who works with whom and how they collaborate is essential context for working autonomously.

Systems thinking includes consideration of all systems that potentially influence or impact the autonomy of your project work. Stakeholder and work systems are many, and mapping them out with inputs and outputs will help understand them for aligning work.

Steps to Implement

Consider the following steps to define and implement systems thinking into your organization:

1. Create a worksheet to define your own, stakeholders', collaborators', and partners' workflows and systems. Include their workflows of inputs, outputs, results, integrations to other workflows and systems, and impacts or conflicts expected. Some systems and workflows to consider include:
   - Your organizational systems
   - Personal/individual systems
   - Stakeholders', collaborators', and partners' systems
   - Competitors' systems
   - External forces
2. Make workflows and systems available to all knowledge workers and create a protocol for using them as reference for all work..
3. Reinforce systems thinking in frequent discussions of project status and purpose. Create some recognition of their integration into a project.
4. Check the artifacts of your systems awareness and thinking. Do they create the narrative that you intend?

The LEGO Group was constantly looking for collaborative opportunities to meet new needs. This collaboration required awareness of the systems within which each of these collaborators operated, were influenced, and were influencers.

Recognizing and accommodating the systems in place in the world around it, this family-owned enterprise has never lost the vision of its founder to promote play to everyone in order to develop the capital of children for the benefit of all ages of people.

Artifacts of these systems and collaborative thinking, internal and external to the organization, throughout The LEGO Group's history include:

Internal

Ole Kirk, an independent carpenter, was open to the idea of selling his peripheral products, such as toys, at a Danish trade fair. He considered himself an expert joiner and carpenter but was intrigued by the value of play. He saw a system within children's play and creativity as a future contributor to adult creativity.

As providers of many products, the company decided to focus on one product and make it into a system of play. The LEGO-in-play concept introduced multiple uses and alternative options to streamline operations but expand the value of play in creative ways with the plastic bricks. The foundational plastic brick was thought of as a material for creative building and role playing. Innovation was continuous as new uses of the bricks were developed.

LEGO leaders added the dimension of role play and diverse behaviors into the creative process of building. This dimension of role play integrated the interests of girls into the system of play, representing a combination of buys' and girls' interests that widened the scope of play with its recognition of societal systems.

When layoffs of employees were necessary, LEGO leaders worked with the union leaders to ensure that families were able to stay together, recognizing the importance of family and supporting relationships.

As the largest employer in Billund, many citizens worked for The LEGO Group. The company made many contributions to the city and has a positive narrative in the community.

External

When a bonus was to be awarded, The LEGO Group distributed cash so that the entire town would benefit from the increased spending in their domain.

The founder saw the future as part of his existence and how he could contribute. He was willing to borrow money from various sources, at the risk of his own well-being, to fund his vision. He was always aware of his options within the system within which he lived and worked and thought about how he could make new contributions, no matter the cost.

As a Danish company, The LEGO Group had an opportunity to compete with the German toy companies, which presented the opportunity to grow. The company embraced this opportunity with a systematic understanding of the competition and its own value.

LEGO developed as part of its Billund community, not just considering its individual and internal organization. Recognizing this trend as a system of supply and demand made the toys even more attractive. It helped Ole Kirk and his need to earn enough money to support his growing family. The awareness of the systems around him and his business brought many evolutions of products throughout LEGO's history. When the materials needed to create his toys became scarce, the company shifted to the newest phenomenon, plastics. The LEGO bricks were born.

LEGOs were designed to build a whole town of Billund, recognizing the whole of life and its needs as a community.

The bricks were meant to define the endeavor of raising children as joyous, as opposed to a duty, with the intent of continuous learning through the creative process.

Recognizing the need for adults to be creative, the scale model line provided a tool for adult play and learning.

LEGO leaders saw the opportunity to extend play to families through family LEGO parks and connections to popular movie characters. Fantasy characters, such as those in Star Wars, were important in society, so LEGO maximized that value by partnering to add play, development, and learning to those characters.

As competition grew, it was necessary to find new customers and markets. The company leaders were open to developing partnerships that would add LEGO bricks to others' products in order to add new markets to existing markets. An example of a partnership was McDonald's fast food restaurants. As McDonald's was perceived as a family restaurant, LEGOs partnered to distribute a small package of LEGOs with each Happy Meal®. The families were now being provided a toy to go with their meals. Recognizing McDonald's Happy Meals as part of a family system, LEGO leaders partnered to build awareness of the bricks as a toy within that family system.

Social systems were always on the minds of LEGO company leaders. Changes in culture and thinking brought new opportunities for using the LEGO bricks to promote play. When overextended, leaders would find new opportunities by modifying the vision of the value of play to accommodate a social or cultural trend. As the digital age came about, LEGO leaders partnered with experts at the MIT Media Lab to create a coding addition to LEGOs for using computers to build creatively.

LEGO's evolution followed culture and society, establishing the value of play and development in all aspects of those evolving systems and domains.

Personal Mastery

Individual personal mastery is defined as achievement in four categories: personal, professional, community, and a domain of expertise. Individuals define goals to establish their paths to mastery in each category and to guide their work and aspirations. The goals are based on individual mindsets, idealized design for the future, invisible capital, and current work. The personal mastery plan is recorded in a personal profile document. This plan is focused on individual development and growth in the context of the organization. Often opportunities for growth are found within the systems that touch workers.

Personal mastery and development build self-confidence, self-accountability, and self-sufficiency to be in control of work and decisions.

Steps to Implement

Consider the following steps to define and implement personal mastery into your organization:

1. All workers build a personal profile that includes mindset, development planning, and a record of all activity, experiences, and achievements. It also includes a description of vision for the future, invisible capital, membership in associations, and network of subject-matter experts. Regular and routine review of personal profiles is important.
2. The personal profiles should be created and available to all in the organization for reference and availability for relevant project work.
3. Define and build mentoring, succession planning, and reskilling programs to support individuals and their pursuit of their development plans.
4. Define and implement a recognition and rewards program to be held routinely and for all workers to participate, as awardees, contributors, or evaluators.

5. Reinforce personal mastery in frequent discussions of project status and purpose. Create some recognition of its contribution to a project.
6. Check the artifacts of personal mastery. Do they create the narrative that you intend?

LEGO ensures that the organization's leaders and employees have a sustainable life and security for personal and professional growth, community engagement, and evolving individual expertise.

The LEGO Group has a unique focus on the quality of their products, including the effort and materials needed to produce this quality. This focus extends to employees, leaders, and the partnerships that contribute to the mastery needed to produce high quality.

Artifacts of this personal mastery, internal and external to the organization, throughout The LEGO Group's history include:

Internal

Ole Kirk had a persona for making close relationships, faith in the farming community around him, the welfare of his employees, and valuing humanity as a first priority.

Ole Kirk's management expectations were high, including hard work and excellent quality in that work. His thinking was always big, expanding the context of his thinking.

Ole Kirk respected the notion of play and its value by observing his own children and their play. It inspired him to know what was of high value to their development.

Ole Kirk saw play as important as joinery and carpentry, imposing the same high quality on each.

When promoting people to management positions, including his son, he developed a learning path for each so that each individual was prepared to contribute high-quality work and decisions.

Ole Kirk's son, Godtfred, recognized the invisible capital of understanding high quality and the intent to build learning within society. This invisible capital was in his family and company, and he was eager to share it within The LEGO Group, its members, and its products.

Godtfred was open to acquiring new skills and attended a technical assistance program, which offered vast new knowledge and expertise in his current industry. He was also very interested in conversing with outsiders and employees for new ideas as he was always eager to self-teach. He expected employees to have new ideas and to innovate routinely.

Employees were expected to think, innovate, and ask lots of questions as they worked toward the company vision.

Godtfred developed a four-step learning system to guide workers. Step 1 was the learning system for children. Step 2 was the product refined for adults. Step 3 was the product for engineers and architects to use in their work. Step 4 was a global system in which LEGO would influence a world shift in how we think as humans.

When hiring a former priest as a new manager, Godtfred made sure that he would be content, motivated, and satisfied with his new position. His concern was that the man was making the right decision for himself.

Children, their play, and learning were role models for LEGO products, citing the inner child as a driver for relevant product design and development.

Compass management was an approach that moved decision making to lower-level managers, engaging them in decision making and growth opportunities. Decision making was moved to the closest manager or employee to the pending problem. It also reduced the time needed to find consensus on resolving an issue.

When change was needed to sustain the company, leaders looked to make that change within the organization through employee mindsets, support, and actions.

When inertia occurred throughout the company, leaders recognized that the employees had stopped having fun in their work. Fun was the motivator that helped them see the vision to be creative, enthusiastic, and spontaneous in their work.

Kjeld sought his own self-confidence when turning the company over to the next generation of leaders while looking forward to his own efforts to seek out play tactics for the future.

Interest in learning and development structured the underlying intent of the enterprise. Personal mastery was essential to that intent.

External

Ole Kirk Christiansen's interest in the correlation of play and development led him to study child psychologists and their current thinking on learning and development.

Play of the highest and creative quality was important to the evolution of humanity, for children, employees, and customers.

The LEGO Group has multiple awards for its movement into the future. Awards were voted on by industry executives and were found meaningful for the peer recognition of the company mastery of their vision and the future needs of child's play.

LEGO created the LEGO prize to recognize efforts, to support work and endeavors, and to contribute to children's lives across the world.

The product, Mindstorms, was developed to enable the LEGO bricks with computers in the digital age, hoping to enhance relevant learning as technology evolved.

New challenges of making bricks relevant in the digital age sparked the development of 3D design for building with bricks on a computer. This development kept employees engaged and invigorated to work toward the company vision of play.

Growth initiatives were often spearheaded and mentored by old friends and acquaintances of company founders, not sought outside and foreign to the company.

The product, Mindstorms, was developed to enable the LEGO bricks with computers in the digital age, hoping to enhance relevant learning as technology evolved.

Shared Vision

The organization's vision is a desired future state that the founders strive to create. Organizations have mindsets that guide workers and work in the common direction of that vision. This vision and mindset are fundamental to the organization, all work, its members, and its success.

The organization's shared vision and mindset should be available for all workers to reference, as needed. This documentation can also include examples of projects, behaviors, and decisions that demonstrate an organization's vision and history. An organization's vision can also include an environment and mode of work that builds worker autonomy and growth. This vision and environment would contribute greatly to the organization's narrative as a good place to work.

Steps to Implement

Consider the following steps to define and implement shared vision into your organization:

1. Define the organization's vision and mindset to support it. The mindset will include the goals, values, beliefs, and mode of work. Include important values of trust, advocacy, specific roles for leaders and workers, budget sharing, and a *Reflections* team.
2. Define approaches for building each of these values.
3. Document and share this information in an accessible way for all members to reference.

4. Allocate time for workers to ponder and discuss the organization's vision and mission.

5. Require workers to apply and record the shared vision and mindset within their work plans and documentation of project work and results.

6. Reinforce the shared vision in frequent discussions of project status and purpose. Create some recognition of its contribution to a project.

7. Check the artifacts of shared vision within your workers and their activities. Do they create the narrative that you intend?

LEGO's shared vision ensures that all members of an organization are aware of and understand the organization's vision as it evolves throughout the organization's history. Shared vision also expects all workers to align and enhance that vision.

LEGO's foundational thinking recognized the value of play, even when the business was about joinery and carpentry for building houses, barns, and so on. The initial distraction of crafting toys was strong and became LEGO's official value being created. LEGO's focus on woodworking evolved to the value of learning and development through play with the small bricks. The innovation and creativity of building to spark creativity was made possible by these small bricks.

Shared vision is probably the most powerful of all organizational elements of a learning organization. Sharing your intended direction based on trends, industry events, and global conditions builds credibility, reliability, and trust.

Artifacts of this shared vision, internal and external to the organization, throughout The LEGO Group's history include:

Internal

Ole Kirk Christiansen shared his thoughts on play and children openly. All of his family and employees knew of his passion for toys and the development process.

Trust and shared vision were widespread in Billund, with most families having someone employed with the company.

The Billund factory had a devastating fire with an aftermath of new building activity that demonstrated loyalty to employees.

The shared vision became a story of how a family used the bricks to tell its family story that could be passed down through generations and their play.

Godtfred initiated a unique managers' approach to reinforce the shared vision of the company with employees. Mistakes were congratulated for their initiative in the pursuit of the vision. There was no fear of failure in any innovative pursuit.

Employees were empowered to work independently all week after a brief meeting on Monday to discuss the work of the week. There were no schedules, only personal intuition and initiative to guide the work.

Godtfred shared his idea of preparing children for life, developing the joy of creativity in everyone.

Worth Knowing *was a series of evening events held to build cohesion among middle managers to support a common approach to management and decision making. Motivation of employees around the shared vision was the purpose of this approach.*

When taking over management, Kjeld wanted to focus on the LEGO soul and what the family wanted to do with the company, as opposed to the use of more tangible words and concepts for growth.

Leaders partnered with education experts to be sure that the shared vision was credible and reliable in guiding the system of play for positive outcomes of development and learning.

Godtfred and Kjeld disagreed on how to pursue future opportunities, but they shared the vision that they had to be in control of that growth, not allowing the new and current markets dictate that growth.

When the communication of Kjeld's shared and evolving vision was challenged with confusion, the company leaders developed a pamphlet to explain in a tangible way. His intent for the future of the company was miles beyond others' thoughts, and he wanted to ensure its clarity for members' understanding and benefit.

Kjeld's vision was foreign to many as it was not about company growth or markets, but it was about how he wanted to contribute to the outside world and to his employees.

The company's inheritance was focused on the shared and evolving vision of the founders. It was not about company ownership, finances, size, or control of the company.

External

Ole Kirk had an entrepreneurial spirit around the introduction of plastics and its use for delivering toys. He further refined his vision of toys when he saw the plastic bricks that came from England.

As these new plastic toys needed a molding machine for production, factory employees were involved in the evolving vision of using the plastic bricks to motivate children's learning and development. "Play well" was introduced as the new vision of the company.

LEGO's diverse set of toys, wooden and plastic, was displayed at an exhibition in 1951. A wooden motor mounted on the back of a boy's bicycle demonstrated the company's evolution into the future. It also reinforced the value of realistic play by providing a driver's license and petrol to replicate the reality of moped riding.

Ole Kirk shared his vision of a system of play with adults. He invited them outdoors to play with their children, capitalizing on the trend of establishing the importance of play to a child's development. He helped establish and reinforce the age of the child with the adults who bought toys for their children.

Ole Kirk shared his idea that play led to active and creative adults.

Godtfred made a massive investment in the rollout of the LEGO system-in-play.

Exported products were modified to accommodate foreign needs and cultures to ensure that the LEGO vision was communicated effectively.

LEGO conferences were held with the intent of building the community of LEGO users from foreign countries. The combination of these attendees was meant to build the shared vision.

The company shared its vision of role play with the production of Minifigures to make play closer to the reality of people and their lives, behaviors, and feelings. This expanded vision included how girls play with how boys play.

Developing a child's imagination was the intent of the vision of having the highest, most valued brand for families with children.

The entire world was to think of The LEGO Group as committed to the best quality and the best toys to incite learning and development of children as the purpose of the company's existence.

Mental Models

Mental models are specific to an organization, its vision, and its mindset. Consider mental models as the common platform of goals, values, beliefs, and mode of work that guides all work and decisions. These mental models give context for how work will be done, leading to little conflict, ease of decision making, and a consistent focus on a common goal. Work and decisions need to align to these goals, values, beliefs, and mode of work for best individual productivity and perform-ance of the organization. When working with colleagues, stakeholders, and partners, it is important that all agree on the same mental models to frame work and decisions in a consistent manner.

Mental models in an autonomous environment might include a service orientation; supply and demand matches; inquiry and learning focus; making decisions, results, and persistence; social engagement; awareness of behavioral tendencies; management theories; retaining workers and customers; and reinforcing autonomy.

Steps to Implement

Consider the following steps to define and implement mental models into your organization:

1. Build a service orientation through examples of serving customers, workers, and collaborators. Recognize and reward instances of service as they occur. Include these stories in a company history with availability to all members.
2. Hold supply and demand discussion forums to observe the decision factors and discuss management of these factors as tangible and intangible for agreement.
3. Hold inquiry and learning discussions to clarify the most feasible path to agreement, including archetype workflow analysis, decision influencers, and choice architectures.
4. Hold review sessions for decision-making processes, including persistence and achieving a result. Discuss behavioral tendencies and management theories as they apply to decisions.
5. Plan social engagements that encourage relationship development among workers.
6. Define and implement a recognition and rewards program to reinforce autonomous behaviors and work. Consider the seven autonomous skills and observe their use during project work of the learning system steps.
7. Plan to recognize and reward efforts to retain a customer or peer worker.

8. Reinforce mental models in frequent discussions of project status and purpose. Create some recognition of their contributions to a project.
9. Check the artifacts of your specific mental models and rate their effectiveness. Do they create the narrative that you intend?

LEGO's mental models engage all organizational members in current and evolving conditions, goals, beliefs, and work processes to support the shared vision of the organization.

LEGO's foundational thinking recognizes the value of people first. That thinking considers good and trustful working conditions for employees, support for the inner self, and the learning and development of children as key to active and creative adult contributors to society. Leaders and workers demonstrate that thinking with all interactions between people and products.

Mental models are the biases or beliefs that employees, customers, and industries hold as the narrative that describes why they should interact with the company.

Artifacts of these mental models, internal and external to the organization, throughout the LEGO Group's history include:

Internal

No matter how disastrous things seemed, Ole Kirk always had faith in the future. Persisting in dark times demonstrated his faith that things will be alright eventually. Forging ahead was his mode and style of life.

After a fire that destroyed the factory, Ole Kirk demonstrated his care for his employees and family by building the new factory next to his personal garden so that employees and family could relax in the garden during work breaks.

LEGO had to think with a strategic and international mindset if it wanted to provide its toys and their benefits beyond their Danish market environment.

Company leaders wanted to share the LEGO model of toys and thinking as extensively as possible. They displayed their toy systems in store windows for all to see and appreciate.

Work, as stimulated with the LEGO system-in-play, promotes creativity, interaction, and quality standards among co-workers and partners from outside organizations.

Godtfred and Ole Kirk had a belief in taking initiative. One learns from just doing something. Employees were rewarded for taking this belief seriously.

When growth was high, confusion and disengagement resulted from many new hires being added to the employee base. A new manager was hired to build new personnel policies to improve work and alignment to LEGO culture and values.

Company belief in the value of diversity led to hiring from other industries.

A new personnel manager championed the LEGO spirit in an employee magazine.

The LEGO Group was determined to view new technologies as tools and would only integrate those tools as necessary to further the system-in-play concept of the bricks.

Per Sorensen, a LEGO manager, held the belief that all situations had to be considered from two diverse perspectives. The leader must take the lead and then recede into the background.

When innovation had slowed, the LEGO leaders created a proactive management course to unleash some of the energy that had become dormant in the workforce. Initiative and innovation had to be rejuvenated. Individual managers had to create the change necessary from within the organization.

A fitness program called attention to fixing today's problem and getting ready for the scenarios of tomorrow simultaneously.

Even in the case of potential layoffs, employees felt solidarity, good will, and support for the founders of The LEGO Group.

Father and son disagreed on the pace of adding products and expanding the company but deferred to one another, as needed, to keep the company moving into the future.

External

Yoyos, a favorite toy, was valued by children and adults alike, demonstrating the inner child in all of us that recognizes the joy in play. LEGO adopted this toy.

Parents' desire to protect their children during societal disasters supported a huge increase in toy sales for LEGO. This trend validated LEGO's value for children's play.

When trade restrictions were going to be lifted, Danish toy companies might succumb to the German industry leaders. Godtfred believed in LEGO and its ability to competitively enter the German market. He persisted by pursuing a special toy, the peace pistol, to compete in that market.

Godtfred's belief in healthy play aligned him and LEGO products to the current trend of the need for good toys, noted by the child psychologists and education experts on the pedagogy of the times.

Bonding and rebuilding of countries after World War II was supported by LEGO with its system of play to create and integrate thinking with others.

LEGO believes in creating toys with long-term benefit and the best systems of play.

As managers had always been male, a female component needed to be added to integrate a feminine voice in decisions and toy development.

With the digital age came passive play. LEGO saw the need to motivate play for growth, socializing, and creativity.

Team Learning

Often twenty-first century work is done in a team structure, and each member of the team has autonomous responsibilities as specific roles require. Collaboration is always needed for agreement, expertise, and availability of resources. In all cases, collaboration is learning-oriented and predominant in an autonomous mode of work. Mindset analysis is necessary for joint decision making.

Teams create a framework to enable team work, inquiry, research, analysis, and learning to ensure consistent and continuous progress. This framework consists of several factors: the other learning organization components; metrics; inquiry, research, and analyses using a digital nervous system of data and information; tools for configuring work and analyses; techniques and protocols to guide work and make decisions; LS; and reflection, recognition, and rewards for autonomous work and results.

Steps to Implement

Consider the following steps to define and implement team learning into your organization:

1. Ensure that the other learning organization components are defined and available to all workers to provide preparation and background for team learning. They frame the mindset of all workers.
2. Define metrics to give context and goals for all work and what it should achieve. Measures can be performance or learning-orien-ted.

3. Set structures and protocols to guide inquiry, research, and analysis for learning and decision making using available data and information.

4. Set protocols for communications and decision making.

5. Expect data-driven learning and decisions.

6. Provide templates to guide team and project charter definitions, as well as team and project activity and results.

7. Define a learning system to consistently guide project work with autonomous skills.

8. Create a *Reflections* team to discuss work, its results, recognition, and rewards for excellence. Discussion of needed improvements and new opportunities uncovered should be held routinely. A regular review of learning organization components is also important to ensure that your autonomous environment is still effective.

9. Reinforce team learning in frequent discussions of project status and purpose. Create some recognition of its contribution to a project.

10. Check the artifacts of team learning and rate their effectiveness. Do they create the narrative that you intend?

Does learning always drive your work and pursuits?

LEGO builds a common platform for learning from team efforts, partner needs, and external experiences.

LEGO's foundational thinking recognized team work and collaboration within and external to the company. The vision of the system of play drove all activity and decisions, both internally in the employee base and outside the company with whomever and whatever held new information and knowledge to drive expansion and accommodation of world needs. Team learning expands thinking internally based on exploration with potential partners, trends, and events in society.

Artifacts of this learning, internal and external to the organization, throughout The LEGO Group's history include:

Internal

Connections to various partners and markets help the design and presentation of new toys.

Leaders learn from each other and accommodate their varying mindsets of company management.

Team learning built trust and openness to be a "we" company. Intentionally getting to know foreign company partners brought them into the "we" paradigm, as well.

Ole Kirk's paradigm of people as opposed to workers created an environment of openness, caring, and learning throughout the company operations.

Innovation is rewarded in the Product Development division.

Systems of play provide inroads into new industry needs in the area of play.

Individual learning and innovation are encouraged and rewarded.

Management practices are regularly updated to align to current employee and innovation needs.

External

Awareness of the German toy market and mindset led to development of competitive toys and advertising.

Partnering with another company led to the realization that wholesalers were not a desirable factor in these transactions.

Computer and digital games introduced product development to the simultaneous use of bricks with the technology, shifting play to a digital version.

Checking the Artifacts of the Project Narrative

Artifacts of your work create the narrative that will engage and encourage others to work with you and your organization. Awareness of these artifacts and their messages to colleagues, stakeholders, and the world will give you the opportunity to control these artifacts to serve you well.

> *LEGO founders, managers, and workers created credible artifacts of their autonomy with their internal operations and with the world as it exists at any point in time. Their worldwide reputation for quality and innovation has built a narrative as they wanted it to be.*

Chapter Summary

This chapter describes what organizational leaders need to consider when building an autonomous environment to meet the needs of their autonomous workers. The next chapter, "Reflections on Artifacts and Narratives," describes the artifacts and resulting narrative of an autonomous learning organization and its autonomous workers.

PART 3

Checking on Autonomy, Environment, and Satisfaction

CHAPTER 7

Reflections on Artifacts and Narratives

"Mayo Clinic is honored to once again lead in more specialties than any other hospital. This recognition affirms our commitment to health-care excellence as we continue to globally transform healthcare for people everywhere." (Gianrico Farrugia, MD, Mayo Clinic's president and CEO)

For over 100 years, the Mayo Clinic has been balancing its values of "patient first" with its strategy of exceptional medical care, medical research, and medical education. The founders think of medical care as that of an engineer mixed with an artist. The engineer is the medical expert for diagnosing and treating patients, while the artist takes care of the mode of delivery to comfort the patient. Multiple doctors collaborate in the treatment of each patient.

The Mayo brothers integrated management with governance in a teamwork approach with all contributing doctors working at the Clinic. They created partnerships in income, in a Mayo Properties Association, a transition to a Board of Governors, and participative governance through committees.

The founder, Dr. William Worrall Mayo, and his sons, Drs. Charles H. Mayo and William J. Mayo, built an exceptional service organization. It is a role model for all service organizations, regardless of industry and specific customers. The Mayo Clinic has become the most influential and valuable service brand in the healthcare industry. Their artifacts are many that have created this narrative. (Berry and Seltman 2008)

Autonomy and learning, a great pair! Intentional learning and how you use it makes you autonomous. There are three critical necessities to building learning. They are (1) a mindset to drive inquiry, (2) reflection that helps evaluate your findings to design change, and (3) using the findings to make change. Reflection is the best path to learning, but only if you intend to use what you learn to make improvements or find new opportunities. Reflection, learning, and change are an important sequence.

A foundational question for reflecting is whether you intend to survive or thrive, as an individual or as an organization. This leads to considerations of development and growth. Development is an incremental plan to improve or seek new opportunities. Growth can result from development but can merely mean more of the same. Developing leads to thriving, while growing may only lead to surviving. Reflection can help you recognize the difference.

Reflecting on the systems that dictate your workflow and outcomes is very helpful. Reflecting on behaviors and decisions that are controlled by your mindset gives clues to your intent to survive or to thrive. Do your behaviors and decisions adapt to survive a conflict or do they generate new opportunities to thrive? When might each approach be relevant? Creating a *Reflections* Team can formalize this process so that routine learning can give insights into when and how to survive and thrive based on past wins and losses.

This chapter discusses reflection and how to use it effectively. Topics include:

- The Value of Reflection
- Surviving Versus Thriving
- Systems
- Behaviors and Decisions
- *Reflections* Team
- The Sequence of Reflections, Learning, and Change
- Chapter Summary

The Value of Reflection

Learning leads to development by creating a path to achieve a goal. Revisiting your mindset to be sure that you are open to learning and acting on your findings is incredibly important. The intentionality to reflect triggers multiple avenues of learning.

Reflecting is the best learning that can be. It is prompted by the readiness of your inquiry. You totally understand the relevance of what you need to understand. You can identify the exact influences that caused an impact. And you are familiar with how you might make a change, when needed. Figure 7.1 describes how reflection supports learning, development, and growth.

Probably most important is the reflection on how your mindset will support your inquiry and learning. Do you value the clarity that comes with learning? Will you be open to the changes that learning suggests? Reflecting with an open mind is the only way to benefit from what you have learned. When you reflect on your previous behaviors, work, and decisions, you will find insights, your own and others, into the rationale that drove them. Once you understand these causes or correlations, you have the ability to make changes to create new outcomes.

Reflecting on goals and values can identify a rationale that caused a situation to occur. If you value your time more than reaching a goal, you will not work with the persistence of unlimited time and effort to reach

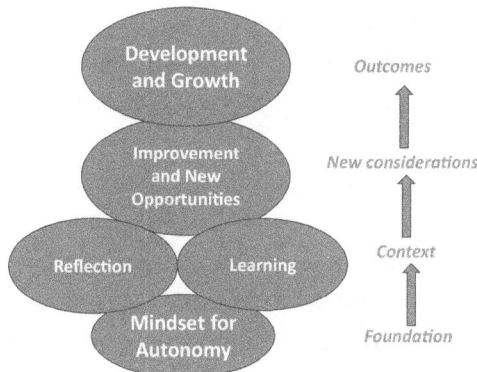

Figure 7.1 Autonomy, Reflection, Learning, Development and Growth

your goal. Are you focused on development for growth or on status quo in life? If you are focused on status quo for a comfortable existence, then you will not pursue a career path that may cause stress or struggle. This would lead to behaviors that adapt to a conflict as opposed to behaviors to generate a new situation to overcome the conflict.

Reflecting on the beliefs and mode of daily work and decisions allows you to see if and how you have supported your goals and values. Are you working in ways that will achieve your goals according to your values? Do you stand firm with your work to align with your goals and values?

Reflection on self is invaluable but doesn't stand alone in seeking to understand an outcome. The mindsets of others and their environments lead to their behaviors, work, and decisions that impact your work and outcomes. People work within the systems that influence and impact them and their mindsets. Reflection is the most effective way to make sense of their behaviors, work, and decisions as guided by their systems and the intentionality of their mindsets.

Aristotle: "The unexamined life is not worth living." (Wargo 2024)

Adaptive Versus Generative Revisions

Work, behaviors, and decisions can adapt to an obstacle or generate a new opportunity through that obstacle. This choice is made by the worker through knowledge of the situation, its potential for creating value, and the effort necessary to generate new value. Adapting to an obstacle may be the most effective approach, such as accommodating another worker's need. Using the obstacle to generate a new product or service is also possible.

Your mindset value for adapting or generating also impacts your decision. Consider that an adaptive approach may be more related to surviving and a generative approach may be more supportive of thriving. When and how do your values support either of these approaches?

Inquiry into your narrative also gives some indication of how your work aligns with the intent of your mindset. What are the artifacts that build your narrative? Recognizing the artifacts of your work is helpful for evaluating your narrative. This narrative, in reflection, demonstrates your intent to survive or thrive, as well as the values that shape your work. This narrative should align with your mindset.

> *Does your work reflect your goals and values? Do you adapt to survive or do you generate to thrive?*

Your Narrative

Your narrative determines whether people want to engage with you. Your narrative defines how you want to be perceived and how you are perceived in the world. If these match, then you have fulfilled the intentionality of your mindset. If they do not match, then an evaluation of each, your mindset and your narrative, is an important topic for reflection. Reflections on what artifacts are creating your narrative is essential. These artifacts make the discussion tangible.

Also, consider that each artifact is interpreted by the mindset of the interpreter. Artifacts are strong signals. You must consider what they mean to you but also what they mean to your stakeholders, collaborators, and partners. A mismatch can be devastating to your narrative, future work, decisions, and results.

Now you can make a plan to modify artifacts, as needed, and your narrative as you wish it to be understood in the world.

The Mayo Clinic is known for its medicine as a cooperative service. A patient is serviced by a primary doctor, who then is responsible for calling in other doctors to collaborate on treatment for the patient. Teamwork is not optional. This cooperative approach is a signal of the comprehensiveness of the service provided.

Surviving Versus Thriving

Reflection is a path to discovering the difference between the intent to survive and/or to thrive. Ackoff, author of *Turning Learning Right Side Up*

(2008), made an interesting distinction that growth and development are very different. One can grow to twice his size with very little development, but development will result in new horizons. Reflection on your development considers your learning, while reflection on your growth may only track your wealth, weight, or number of family members. None of these growth factors necessarily indicate learning and development.

Surviving can happen with growth but thriving happens only through development. Surviving is based on today's needs and what you know today. Thriving can be thought of as forecasting tomorrow's needs through learning, LS systems analyses, and idealized design. These reflections guide you for the purpose of thriving.

Surviving usually comes before thriving and is sometimes necessary before thriving can happen. Reflect on your mindset and what you do. Are your goals always about thriving or always about surviving? Do your goals and metrics indicate survival or new development to thrive?

> *How are you developing for growth?*

When you reflect on these questions, consider your invisible capital and its value to your endeavors, as well as your idealized design of your future. Do your goals consider both of these aspects? They can surely contribute to your surviving and thriving.

Goals come in two formats, learning goals and performance goals. Learning goals define the path of achievements needed to get to your performance goals. Reflect on how you make both of these types of goals and how they impact your work and decisions. You might consider that learning goals are more likely to lead to thriving, while performance goals can be more related to surviving. These premises are not always true but do warrant inspection through reflection.

> *Considering your organization and its mode of work, would you say that surviving or thriving is the intent?*

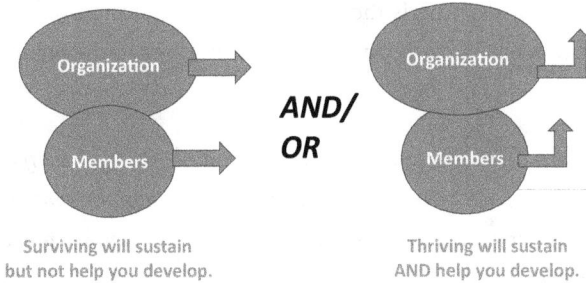

Surviving will sustain
but not help you develop.

Thriving will sustain
AND help you develop.

Figure 7.2 Surviving and Thriving

Any organization most likely needs to survive and thrive. Does your organization blend development and growth perspectives in order to survive and thrive? Growth may indicate more of the same with little intent to develop along the way. This growth may not be adequate to sustain you longer term as changes and challenges are constant.

Development will enhance the autonomy of your organization to focus on thriving. Autonomy unlocks the ability of everyone in your organization to contribute to organizational development for growth along with each individual's development. This means that everyone in the organization is reflecting routinely and intentionally working toward surviving and thriving. Figure 7.2 demonstrates the difference between surviving and thriving.

Learning, development, and growth are opportunities that organizations can provide to their members. Reflecting on how content and motivated members are to develop and grow is a great indicator of their satisfaction and tendency to contribute to the future of the organization. It is important to reflect on their personal mastery, shared vision, and mental models. Do these learning organization components demonstrate artifacts to support the development of the organization? The important question to ask is how satisfied are workers with the vision and mindset of the organization to survive and/or thrive. How does the organization align to workers' needs to develop and grow?

Does your organization and its members strive to survive or thrive?

Surviving or thriving is the result of worker autonomy that leads to their development, growth, and their contributions to the organization.

The Mayo Clinic is focused on thriving with its three artifacts of medical care, research, and education. These divisions complement each other in a comprehensive approach to the service they provide to their patients.

Systems

Systems are cycles of work and interdependence. This interdependence happens when stakeholders and collaborators work together. Reflecting on all of these systems, their connections, and interdependencies identifies inefficiencies, obstacles, and new opportunities. Systems are everywhere and are influential in how work gets done. The systems of an organization influence work internally and are influenced by external systems, as well. Work within systems is defined by the organizational mindset. Reflection builds awareness of these systems and mindsets as influencers to your work and workers.

Operational Systems

Reflecting on the use and outcomes of operational systems makes it easy to see where an obstacle or conflict occurred as these systems create routines that are easy to track.

Examples of operational systems that warrant reflection include:

- *Supply and Demand Factors*–Define cause and effect to indicate the ability to match supply and demand decisions of workflow.
- *Learning Organization*–Define how the five organizational elements of systems thinking, personal mastery, shared vision, mental models, and team learning work together to support autonomous work.
- *Learning System (LS)*–Define how the six steps of the LS align their inputs and outcomes to achieve success in work.

- ***Operational Structures*–**Define how metrics, tools, techniques, and protocols influence work and workers.
- Metrics include the defined expected outcome of a project, effort, or work and how this expected outcome is to be measured.
- Tools are resources, such as LS steps, data and information sources, and template formats for guiding work.
- Techniques include decision-making parameters, communications, analytic methods, and using the seven skills of autonomy.
- Protocols are the nuances of how techniques are used consistently, including decision responsibility, communications frameworks, innovation standards, and resource allocations.

> *Do your operational structures define and support autonomy within your organization? Do they support development and/or growth?*

Systems Archetypes of Workflows

Senge (1990) defines ten archetypes of workflow that help you understand positive and negative outcomes of work. Archetype workflows define specific work steps that align inputs and outcomes. Reflecting on these possible workflows gives insights into obstacles, unrealistic goals, or worker mindset conflicts. When workers have these insights, they can work more effectively to counter negative or support positive outcomes. They can foster agreement on next steps, which make critical decisions collaborative. Relevant archetype systems can be defined as needed for your work and workers. When workers are trusted to analyze archetype workflows and determine next steps, they are more likely to work autonomously.

> *Do you and your workers consider archetypes and how to manage for positive outcomes?*

Create and consider workflow archetypes to evaluate your project work and decisions:

1. What are your relevant archetypes or models of workflows?
2. Where does your work deviate from a standard archetype workflow?
3. Who are the stakeholders in this workflow?
4. What needs to change to reach the intended outcome or your workflow?

Systems of Trends and Events

Peter Drucker, author of *Innovation and Entrepreneurship* (1985), identifies seven possibilities to frame new opportunities. These paths to new value can be explored using analysis tools of *brainstorming, brain steering, and mind mapping.* These possibilities for creating new value include:

- *Unexpected Success or Failure*–Catalyst to root-cause analysis to identify new or existing need
- *Incongruities*–Discrepancy between what is and what ought to be or between what is and what people assume to be
- *Process Need*–Improve an existing process, replace a weak link, redesign for greater efficiency
- *Industry and Market Structures*–National to global presence, new technology impacts
- *Demographics*–Social, philosophical, political, and intellectual environment changes
- *Changes in Perception*–Fad or trend? New awareness of a need
- *New Knowledge*–Combination of knowledge coming together, when a new idea finally takes hold.

Reflections on current work and projects can be framed with these possibilities for uncovering potential opportunities.

General Systems Topics for Reflection

Reflecting happens routinely and as a habit before and after each behavior, action, and decision. Reflecting to identify what came before to cause an outcome and what comes after to provide input to the next step in the workflow is helpful in predicting the next step results. This is the ultimate learning system of autonomy. Consider each of the following systems to reflect on the causes and effects of outcomes:

- Current resources in the context of current and new projects
- Worker preparation, perspectives, and suggestions
- Failures and their causes and/or correlations
- Organizational conditions and any infrastructure obstacles

Mayo's systems are extensive, bringing doctors, patients, and care into one flow of quality service. All contributors understand and adhere to the standards of expected service and the "patient first" philosophy.

The Mayo Clinic has evolved with four steps to build the organizational systems that differentiate it today. These steps were implemented incrementally and include: (1) doctor's service income versus asset income, (2) non-profit status to promote and invest in research and education, (3) structures to support team-based medical practices, such as a common medical record, and (4) committee management to look after of the many aspects of the Clinic and train staff members on understanding management and business domains. Understanding this evolution of development provides insight into how the Mayo founders and doctors built a widely recognized and exceptional service organization. This service is understood to be internal and external to their contributors and the domain of healthcare competence. Reflecting on the importance and relevance of these services leads to their further evolution to sustain their narrative for excellence.

Behaviors and Decisions

Reflecting on behaviors and decisions leads to the cause and effect of outcomes. This reflection builds awareness of decision factors for matching supply, demand, mindset awareness, and needs.

The LEGO Group has reflection built into its fiber. External awareness of societal needs, environments, competitors, and markets was the result of continuous reflection. This reflection was done by the company leaders to create new strategies for the company to thrive. It was also done by the workers who were expected to find new ideas for efficiency and new innovations as they worked. This continuous reflecting ensured that the company was on a path for continuous development of new markets, partners, and worker satisfaction. Status quo was never acceptable. Workers understood this mindset and contributed to it as often as they could.

Analytic tools can structure this reflection, starting with the *Five Whys* approach to identify the motivators of a behavior, action, or decision. This creates an understanding of cause and effect, as well as the correlation between actions and outcomes. What you learn from this *Five Whys* analysis can lead to an opportunity to improve or completely change your outcome. Structured reflection is key to consistently correcting mistakes and achieving goals. Economists agree that people make choices to satisfy their needs. These choices are complex and dependent upon multiple tangible and intangible factors for suppliers and demanders to understand each other's needs.

It is important to evaluate your problem-solving as adaptive or generative. Either approach may be relevant depending on the situation, but it is good to be aware of how you are inclined to manage issues.

Inquiry Into Mindsets

Another valuable reflection is delving into the mindsets of all contributors to work. Consider how your organizational mindset of goals, values, beliefs, and mode of work support autonomy and development. How do your leaders and workers align with that mindset? Are there some diverse thoughts in their mindsets that should be considered within your organizational mindset? If workers believe that only local work is beneficial, how would that influence your organizational mindset? Do the workers need to modify their beliefs? If mindsets don't match, they must be refined to create a common platform of goals, values, beliefs, and mode of work. Reflect on each mindset within your world of work, including leaders, workers, and partners for a match. Mindsets are

REFLECTIONS ON ARTIFACTS AND NARRATIVES   165

responsible for behavioral tendencies, which are invaluable to uncover when trying to find a cause or correlation for a mismatch of supply and demand.

Encourage workers to personally reflect on their mindsets and how their behaviors, work, and decisions contribute to their individual development and growth. Do behaviors, work, and decisions support their mindsets? Individuals can also reflect on how their mindsets align with their organization's mindset.

Jill and Jim reflected mostly on the approval and acceptance of all stakeholders and contributors to their documentation project. They were well aware of the potential obstacles they could face and reflected step-by-step to ensure that obstacles or gaps were anticipated with inquiry, communication, and celebration of results as they met the project goals. Reflecting for Jill and Jim meant being aware of all needs and fulfilling them before they became problematic. This reflecting was reminiscent of other work experiences that gave context to their current work and the workers involved in the project and its outcomes.

Leaders and Management Theories

Reflecting on how managers use the three options of management theories, including *Theory X* for giving workers direction, *Theory Y* for promoting worker self-direction, or *Theory Z*, focusing on worker self-development, provides insights into how leaders are reinforcing autonomous behaviors, work, and decisions. How and when do leaders take control, give control, and encourage individual development in their management of situations and workers?

Each of these approaches can be applied situationally to lead the organization to autonomy.

What do workers say about the mode of management within your organization?

Personal and Individual Reflections on Satisfaction

Individuals can reflect on their personal mastery. Are personal profiles and development plans current? Are plans being fulfilled to create contentment, motivation, and satisfaction? Every organizational member should have a plan and path to satisfaction with an individual mindset and development thinking. When this path is weak or not present, satisfaction and autonomy do not exist.

> *Elena, violin protégé, ensured her satisfaction by examining her mindset and its potential to ensure her satisfaction. Her goals and value were both helpful to her as she reflected to find a new path to align them to satisfy her.*

Reflection on this profile and development plan should be encouraged on a routine basis.

Inquiry Into Leaders' and Workers' Trust for Each Other

Trust is a very important element of an autonomous organization. Reflecting on trust levels between leaders and workers in both directions gives important insights into organizational autonomy and performance. What demonstrates trust within your organization? Without the trust of leaders by workers and of workers by leaders, autonomy cannot exist.

> *Do leaders and workers discuss trust among themselves?*

Your Organizational Mindset

> *Is your organizational mindset setting up and supporting autonomy within your organization?*

A reflection on the vision, goals, values, beliefs, and mode of work of your organization is very insightful. Does the work of your projects reflect this vision and mindset? Do workers reflect the vision and mindset when planning and expecting results? Does any aspect of your vision and mindset create an obstacle to worker autonomy?

Quality of care and service are top priorities at The Mayo Clinic. The artifacts of that quality extend to all signs inside and outside of the organization. A lab technician was chastised for having dirty shoelaces as they do not signal the highest of quality to external observers. All clues in the domain of the Clinic must demonstrate confidence in this level of quality. Patients have experiences that must match this quality in all regards.

Reflections Team

As has been previously discussed, a *Reflections* team keeps reflection current in an organization. This team creates a formal structure for communicating about improving current work and outcomes, potential new value, quantifying and qualifying that value, and prioritizing it with other opportunities. And most importantly, it reinforces the practices of reflection.

This team holds regularly scheduled discussion sessions to consider and reflect on inquiries, ideas, and analyses, including all of the topics noted in this chapter in separate sessions. Discussions include all outcomes of work, wins, losses, and opportunities presented with a routine process of reflection. Attendance at discussions should be optional and open to all members, as they wish to learn and contribute to the conversation. Supporting a routine reflection process involving all work and its systems will likely lead to many opportunities for consideration.

An autonomous environment encourages reflection at every step in the work, learning, and development path. Recognize that reflection is probably the most helpful of all autonomous skills to lead you to success and control of your life and your organization.

Observing and reflecting on the world around you often offer opportunities. The world is constantly changing, as are the industries, customers, systems, and environments that impact your work and outcomes. Adam Grant, author of *Think Again* (2021), considers reflection as a way to uncover biases that can obstruct progress. Reflecting on why you think what you think and how you might think differently can lead to uncovering a new mode of work or opportunity that is currently in your midst. Checking in on mindset components can also lead to rethinking a belief or goal that might be obscuring your view of an opportunity. Reflecting sees obstacles and opportunities in the context of your mindset. Also, considering another's mindset can present new thoughts to suggest modification to your own mindset.

> *Is your mindset derailing you or propelling you when reflecting on current, previous, and future work?*

The Sequence of Reflection, Learning, and Change

Reflection leads to learning and learning can lead to change. A commitment to considering and using that learning to modify work or a mindset is the most important part of reflection. When reflection yields new thinking, actions, behaviors, and decisions, it has fulfilled its purpose. Otherwise, reflection can be a frustration for those involved.

This sequence can be facilitated by structured analyses of ideas to consider their value to individuals or the organization.

> *The doctors at Mayo plan for continued quality into the future of their service to patients. When one specialty area lost money for 2 years in a row, inquiry into the cause reflected that hospital stays were longer than planned and that multiple implant types were used for similar surgery purposes. Each had caused unnecessary expenses. Changes would have to be made.*

Chapter Summary

This chapter describes the value of reflection, areas of reflection, and resulting organizational change, as needed, to ensure successful and value-creating work. It also discusses the need for a positive narrative and how reflection can help create that narrative. The next chapter, "Uncertainties, Satisfaction with Autonomy," describes the need to satisfy workers through their contentment and motivation, which are individually defined by the autonomous worker.

CHAPTER 8

Uncertainties, Satisfaction with Autonomy

As you recall, Josh is the owner of a landscaping company and noticed that his second and third locations were not as productive as his first location. Josh paid workers a percentage of new business revenues based on their referrals. However, there were many more referrals in the first location than in the second and third. When he asked his workers to create personal profiles to plan their development and futures, he knew from his research that workers needed to be content but also motivated to develop their skills to grow themselves and their organizations. Perhaps the profiles would give him some insights into how his workers were thinking. He found uncertainty among his workers. They were not clear on their responsibilities, the extent of their commitment to customers, and who was in charge of the work being done. They were content with their pay and benefits but couldn't be motivated to bring in new business because they were unsure of Josh's intent for their futures and how advancement might happen. They were also unsure of Josh's vision and mindset for the future of the landscaping business. Josh was really happy to have this insight and started to build his vision and mindset for the business. He wanted to share it with his workers as a basis for how and what they might expect to contribute to that vision and their own development.

The uncertainty of twenty-first century conditions causes discomfort and fear. Workers cannot do their best work if they are distracted by this uncertainty in the world and in their workplaces. This uncertainty or lack of satisfaction can cause quiet quitting. Systematically tending to workers satisfaction is one of the most important focuses of leaders in organizations today. Understanding the relevant needs of these workers allows leaders to create the environments needed for workers to build their satisfaction. When organizations create an environment for them to pursue their destinies, they are sure to be satisfied with their work and lives.

Workers are the most important and valued asset of any organization. Their satisfaction is key to maintaining their value to an organization and to themselves. It means that they are content with their work situation and motivated to grow within and with the organization. Creating an environment to help them be content and motivated will lead to their satisfaction and outstanding performance in an organization. Continuous reflection on behaviors, work, and decisions can evaluate the conditions of the organization that prompts this contentment and motivation for building worker satisfaction.

This chapter discusses contentment, motivation, and satisfaction of workers. Recognizing that workers are the catalyst of success and value for all, it is essential to build an environment that integrates organizational goals, societal responsibility, and individual contentment and motivation. Topics include the following:

- Twenty-first Century Workers
- Satisfaction Defined
- Contentment
- Motivation
- Managing Satisfaction
- Checking the Artifacts of Your Narrative
- Chapter Summary

Twenty-first Century Workers

Twenty-first century trends have had significant impacts on work and workers, who have often responded with quiet quitting. When workers quietly quit, leaders need to evaluate the causes and remedy the situation by helping these workers define what will satisfy them and then work toward that satisfaction. Autonomous workers define these scenarios through their mindsets of agency, finding options, and taking control of decisions. Also, this satisfaction will meet organizational needs, as well.

Quiet Quitting

Unfortunately, the twenty-first century trend of quiet quitting has relegated approximately 50 percent (Gallup 2022) of workers to a lack of workplace and work engagement, based on over 15,000 full- and part-time U.S. employees surveyed, aged 18 and over. These workers are doing as little as possible to fulfill their work requirements, with no extra effort to develop or grow, for themselves or for their organizations. Understanding individuals and their needs, as described in personal profiles and their mindsets, provides insights into their needs and behaviors. Job satisfaction can most assuredly change this trend of quiet quitting by building contentment and motivation.

> As Josh shared his vision and mindset for the company, his workers now had an idea of the future of the business and potential roles for themselves in that future. Jack also found that some workers were more content and motivated than others. He decided to make development and growth plans with each worker to match their individual needs.

Quiet Committing

Managers are essential to combatting quiet quitting with quiet committing. David Brooks (2024b), *New York Times* opinion contributor, cites the importance of middle managers and their commitment to worker satisfaction. Middle managers are the bridge that connects workers to their organizations and the development of both. Unfortunately, again, managers have the greatest drop in work engagement. This drop impacts workers' need for clarity of work expectations, opportunities to learn and grow, feeling tended as a person, and connecting to the organization's mindset. Less than 40 percent of young workers are clear on what is expected of them. Managers need to be reskilled to build the work environment that serves workers who need their attention and help. Meaningful communications on an intentional and frequent schedule will begin to build the trust needed for workers to build their autonomy which will lead to their satisfaction. Workers have to be able to connect their work to the purpose and mindset of the organization, as well as to their own development and growth.

Managers must quietly commit to building contentment and motivation to engage and satisfy workers for highest performance. Understanding individuals and their needs, as described in personal profiles and development plans, can help managers create the environment that will satisfy workers.

> *Josh helped each worker identify current and future needs. His business was small, so he and each worker had to be creative in identifying development opportunities that were attractive to each. Creative discussion was insightful into worker's interests and strengths, as well as opportunities for the business to develop and grow. The timeline of each development plan was specific to each worker's personal and professional needs.*

> *Jack was building trust individually with each worker. He had a plan with each worker for contentment and motivation toward building each worker's future and the landscaping business together.*

In an interview with Karen Mangia, *Authority Magazine*, I discussed five commitments that CEOs and managers can make to address the quiet quitting trend. These five commitments include the following:

1. To support employee growth and development planning, goals, and relevant work
2. To recognize and reward employees for good work
3. To continuously and diligently communicate to ensure readiness, relevance, reinforcement, and reflection on current work
4. To support decision making as close as possible to the issue at hand
5. To ensure that resources to support autonomy exist and persist

These five commitments will build trust with workers and help to understand their needs for contentment and motivation. Herzberg (Nickerson 2023), a psychological researcher, identifies and describes the factors of satisfaction as hygiene, meaning contentment, and motivation, leading to development and growth. Hygiene factors consider comfort and discomfort in the work and workplace. Motivational factors consider development and growth that make workers feel good about their work.

Contentment includes the hygiene needs of compensation and security. Motivation includes the tools and opportunities to learn and grow. Satisfaction is managed by organizational members and their leaders. Contentment and motivation should be routinely addressed with specific and individual communication and relevant programming.

> *Autonomous workers are content and motivated in their satisfaction. They have taken control of that satisfaction.*

In the collaborative knowledge economy, compatibility is an important aspect of contentment and motivation. So knowledge workers define their autonomous mindsets to build their contentment and motivation, as well as compatibility with others. Mindset components of goals, values, beliefs, and mode of work should pave the way to building satisfaction by defining the specifics of an individual's contentment, motivation, and compatibility for guiding collaborative work.

It is important to recognize that compatibility will depend on the mindsets of all collaborators and how they align for decision making. Seeking to understand these mindsets is a skill of autonomy and an important factor in building contentment and motivation. Collaborative agreement and achieving desired results are catalysts for maintaining content and motivated workers.

Satisfaction can come from any combination of contentment, motivation, and compatibility that is suited to an individual worker's needs at a point in time. The need to survive or thrive is a good indicator of how a worker might define mindset goals and values to accommodate current needs. You might think of contentment as surviving and motivation as thriving. Both surviving and thriving can be defined within your autonomous mindset. An individual's mindset sets up the goals of contentment and motivation and defines how to pursue these goals for satisfaction and success. Both surviving and thriving are fundamental aspects of autonomy, which lead to individual's growth and contributions to organizational growth.

For example, a young worker with several children might tend to focus more on contentment than on motivation. A mid-level manager, who is ready to advance in position and responsibility as quickly as possible, might focus more on motivational factors.

The contentment or comfort of workers is as important as motivating them toward their individual growth. Both are important aspects of leaders' relationships with workers. Motivation involves the fostering of good will and attention to workers and their development throughout their work. Individuals and organizations develop and grow together. Satisfaction is the combination of contentment and motivation that is defined by each worker to accommodate individual needs at different times and aspects of each's life.

Satisfaction through Autonomy

Satisfaction and autonomy are connected as they serve each other within the organizational systems of work. Autonomous workers have identified the contentment and motivation that will lead to their satisfaction. This autonomy is defined within workers' mindsets and development plans to guide the highest performance for themselves and their organizations. The quest for satisfaction is supported by an autonomous environment that prompts and supports contentment and motivation in work and decisions.

Autonomy puts the individual workers in control of their destinies, guided by their contentment and motivation. Contentment and motivation are defined in their goals and values. They are built through the compatibility and success of their work as guided by their beliefs and mode of work.

The self-confidence of autonomy is grounded in each worker's idealized design of goals, invisible capital, awareness of the organizational mindset, and in the ability to collaborate with others. Along with compensation, safety, and access to supervisor input, self-confidence builds contentment. The self-accountability of autonomy presents the need to find options to solve problems or find new value. The need for options for problem-solving builds worker motivation to seek new value and new opportunities. Worker growth happens through this inquiry and subsequent research. The self-sufficiency of autonomy presents the opportunity to take control of decisions, work toward results, and, subsequently, builds satisfaction.

> *Autonomous workers are content and motivated in their satisfaction. They have taken control of that satisfaction.*

Corporate Social Responsibility

Current-day workers are concerned about social problems and are eager for their employers to take part in solving these problems. Corporate social responsibility (CSR) (Henderson 2018) is a current trend that brings corporations, workers, and society together in pursuit of a better world for all. Engaging workers in societal sustainability, their own growth, and that of their organizations begins to bridge the gap between organizational success, worker satisfaction, and societal needs. Leaders attempt to balance the business interests, the worker interests, and the needs of society. Businesses provide capital and resources. Workers contribute their efforts to the work autonomously. Nonprofit organizations contribute awareness of societal problems and insights into the mindsets of stakeholders involved. Creating a platform for CSR is important to today's workforce. This work is a catalyst to their satisfaction.

Satisfaction Defined

Satisfaction can mean many things to many people. The satisfaction of twenty-first century workers can be complex due to their autonomy and varying values. Organizational leaders have to provide an environment that fosters worker's ability to find satisfaction. Worker satisfaction will retain them and benefit the organization through their motivation to grow themselves and create new value for the organization.

Satisfaction means that workers are content and motivated to deliver on organizational goals, contribute to societal needs, and meet individual needs for development and growth. These three needs describe the agenda of twenty-first century organizations and the environment that they create to satisfy workers. Organizations need to sustain and thrive through their goals, while meeting in some way societal needs, such as climate control, globalization, and technology acceleration. They need to develop workers as autonomous individuals to support these goals.

Each worker defines a personal level of contentment and motivation that will add up to the individual's unique satisfaction. This combination may be different at different stages in a worker's life. Worker satisfaction presumes that the workers will be autonomous in building their contentment and motivation.

Doug, food and farm industry expert, had to help his new workers balance their contentment with their jobs and their motivation to manage new responsibilities as the organization evolved with new partners and customers. Doug ensured that each had a vision and a mindset to work toward that vision, as well as using the context of the organization's vision and plan for success. His shared vision was very helpful to his workers as they built their own visions and mindset for contributing to the organization. The workers and the organization would reach satisfaction together.

The most effective approach for an organization to meet its goals, societal challenges, and worker needs is to prepare workers to build their autonomy to guide meaningful progress in all domains of need. Workers are the dictators of their own satisfaction and work to meet the needs of the organization. They are best served by relying on their own thinking to guide their contentment and motivation. When others define those needs, they may have the best of intentions, but they cannot know the individual as he knows himself.

Leaders say that the challenges of global change require a shift of responsibility from employer to employee. Employers must give people opportunities and tools to succeed, but individuals must keep themselves ready for the future.

IBM created an innovation … to offer incentives for employees to invest in their own continuing education. IBM matches individual contributions into a portable individual savings fund that employees can use to further their education or get training to switch careers, inside or outside of IBM. When CEO Sam Palmisano announced this in a speech in July 2007, he received 2000 emails from IBMers within hours, … orders of magnitude more, he joked, than he would get for a new dental or eyeglass benefit. This is a company match, not an entitlement program, to make clear that individuals must take responsibility to be competitive—personal responsibility is an IBM value. (HBR, Kanter 2009)

Figure 8.1 demonstrates the connections between the levels of autonomy and the levels of satisfaction.

Josh was eager to build workers' satisfaction by expecting autonomy in his workers. He realized that they may be content with their responsibilities, but he had not previously motivated them in meaningful ways to build the customer base. He has been focused on the management of the business and not on the well-being of his workers. His individual planning with each worker required each to define goals and values that would provide motivation and continued contentment. Workers were the best source for uncovering what they need to be satisfied. This planning also included Josh's expectations on acquiring new customers. They started working together to meet each other's needs.

This process began workers' journeys to building their agency, finding options, and taking control of decisions. Josh was helping them become autonomous in their lives and work.

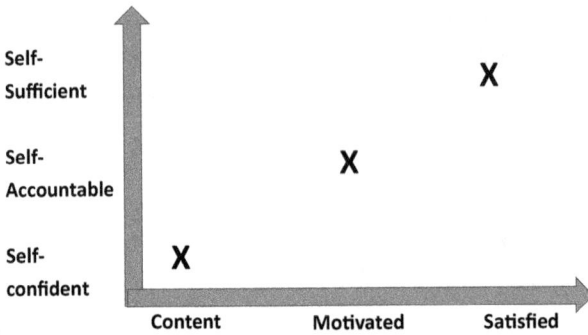

Figure 8.1 Satisfaction and Autonomy

Model for Systematic Development

Usually contentment precedes motivation. Maslow's (Smith 2017) stages of human development include five steps that progress from contentment to motivation. These five stages are incremental, and each must be achieved before the next stage can be pursued. They are a framework for developing autonomy and satisfaction. Consider using these stages as a path to satisfaction. The first three stages of physiology, safety, and belonging lead to contentment. The next two stages of esteem and self-actualization are motivational for achieving goals, development, and growth. This systematic development is helpful to workers as they build their development plans to achieve their goals. This model is also helpful for leaders as they assist workers in their planning and to provide relevant work opportunities. The final stage of self-actualization leads to autonomy and satisfaction.

Contentment

Some women don't ask for pay raises because they're afraid of the consequences but also lack confidence to ask. (Siu 2024)

Contentment is the first step in being satisfied with your work and environment. Herzberg describes contentment to include the hygiene factors that avoid unpleasantness. They include the following:

- *Interpersonal relations*: team versus individual work
- *Salary:* range of compensation based on worker investment in growth
- *Company politics and administration:* worker involvement on committees
- *Supervision:* access to a supervisor and the choice to supervise or mentor another worker
- *Working conditions:* choices of locations and timeliness of meetings

Contentment means being OK with your situation. It can be supported by an individual's personal mastery of an area of expertise and shared vision with the organization. These perspectives give context for finding your contentment, even when a new mode of work is introduced. Working with your individual and organizational perspective provides work security.

Your contentment builds self-confidence to tackle new modes of work and relate to varying management theories, as needed, due to varying scenarios. Managers may be directive, hands-off, or supporting your development and growth. Self-confidence also builds your awareness of how systems work in helping maximize your independent and dependent work. It also brings clarity to team decisions with the self-confidence of expertise, knowledge of other's expertise, and the organization's needs. Work is pleasant, routine, and makes you feel content.

Assessing Hygiene/Contentment Factors

Reflection with workers on their contentment with hygiene factors is a manager's role. Inquiry into their mindsets and needs can help with meeting those needs. It also provides an opportunity for workers to reflect on the relevance of their mindsets and how contentment is actually created.

Inquiry might include the following:

- Describe your team work and individual work. Does it seem to be going well? Do you have any issues or conflicts that could be resolved?
- Is your salary within the range of your expectations? Do you know how and when that salary is managed or increased? What would impact that salary or your salary needs?
- Are you involved in any company committees or special events? Do you have any interests that are not available for you to pursue?
- Do you mentor or supervise another worker? Do you enjoy this activity? Does it help you in any way?
- How is your schedule of work, including your commute, meeting schedule, and timeliness of decision making?
- What might add to your contentment?

Josh scheduled individual meetings with each of his workers to focus on their contentment and how important contentment was to each of them. A few said that contentment was 90 to 100 percent of their satisfaction. The others said that contentment was about 50 percent of their satisfaction and that they wanted opportunities to grow in responsibility and salary. Josh then asked each worker to cite the specifics, or the artifacts, that would make him content.

Motivation

Motivation is the fuel to support development and growth. Motivational factors that make workers feel good about their work are intrinsic to their work. Herzberg's motivational factors include the following:

- *Advancement:* duration of review periods
- *The work itself:* metric and definition of work goals, values, beliefs, and mode of work
- *Possibility for growth:* aspirational levels of advancement
- *Responsibility:* level of decision making
- *Recognition:* regularly scheduled work review
- *Achievement:* goals and work review schedule with metrics

Motivation builds your self-accountability to explore options for solving a problem or finding a new opportunity. Learning components of systems thinking, shared vision, and team learning provide context for identifying and analyzing options and choices to solve a problem. These learning perspectives motivate the workers to see the interdependencies of workflows and diverse mindsets.

Awareness of systems and mindsets is motivational since it provides context for helping to align work of contributors who might differ in their thinking, behaviors, and decisions. Systems thinking enables analysis of this diverse thinking to prompt common thinking for expediting work. Archetype workflow analysis motivates creative thinking to fulfill a need. Awareness of behavioral tendencies and their origins helps to align mindsets for common work.

Motivation has two contexts: (1) your own development and goals and (2) your organization's development and goals. Integrating these two contexts is motivational for finding challenging and growth-oriented initiatives.

Elena, a violin protégé, had ideas on what made her content and what made her motivated. These were defined in her mindset goals and values. Her goal was defined by others in her industry but her values defined another goal for her. She had to reconsider the factors that would lead to her contentment and motivation and rebalance them to adjust her goals based on her values. She valued her family life more than her career goal. This reflection really helped her seek alternate employment as an orchestra leader, as opposed to her previous goal of a soloist career. She was now satisfied with her life.

Assessing Motivation Factors

Leader's reflection with workers on their motivation to learn and grow is insightful. Inquiry into their development plans and needs can help with meeting those needs. It also provides an opportunity for workers to reflect on the relevance of their goals and how motivated they are to pursue and achieve those goals. Managers can add to this reflection with connection to organizational goals.

Inquiry might include the following:

- Do you get feedback as frequently as you would like it to be?
- Do you get meaningful feedback on your mindset and work that supports it?
- Do you aspire to advancement? What does advancement look like to you? Is that advancement available to you?
- Do unexpected opportunities present themselves?
- Is your level of decision making relevant to your expertise and role within the organization?
- Are you recognized for your work as often as you think appropriate to your performance?
- Are your achievements reviewed and rewarded as appropriate to their value?
- What might add to your motivation?

Josh was very curious about the actual areas of motivation that were of interest to his workers. Perhaps they had innovative ideas that would be feasible to pursue. His own ideas on areas of company development were also relevant to align to the motivations of his workers. He planned to seek opportunities for his workers that would support both motivations. To check his understanding of motivational factors, Josh asked each worker to cite the artifacts that would ensure each's motivation.

Managing Satisfaction

Satisfaction results from worker contentment and motivation. Satisfaction builds your self-sufficiency. Satisfaction means that you are content with your hygiene factors and motivated to develop and grow. This combination of contentment and motivation is customized by individual workers, depending on goals and stages of development. Varying levels of contentment and motivation can make up satisfaction. Varying stages of life and responsibility are often catalysts for this combination.

When satisfied, you are in control of your behaviors, work, and decisions.

The state of your organization may also be a factor in your balance of contentment and motivation. Start-ups can offer significant motivation with growth opportunities but less in the area of contentment.

Josh's company was a start-up, so he realized he had to offer opportunities for growth to his workers that would add to their motivation, as he was limited in the compensation he could offer. He could create opportunities for workers to build the company in new and meaningful ways. He created some parameters for expanding the company and was open to discussing all ideas for developing and growing. Josh was seeking to partner with his workers through the trust built with the contentment and motivation of satisfaction.

If you consider the idealized design of your work and organization within the industry and market, relevant opportunities can help define a worker's potential growth trajectory. This trajectory can define an incremental path of combined contentment and motivation. A worker's situation and influencers are critical to understanding contentment and motivators.

Leader's Role in Managing Satisfaction

How do leaders initiate the campaign against quiet quitting toward contentment, motivation, and subsequent job satisfaction? Successful leaders engage with contentment factors. Once contentment is assured, the conversation can shift to future aspirations from the personal profile. Relevant work can be made accessible to achieve those aspirations.

The essential role of the manager's work is to build the trust needed to ensure contentment and collaborate on an individual's development plan for motivation. The manager can help ensure that the plan is feasible and that opportunities are available to meet the defined goals. This work is highly individualized, and therefore, options need to be available to meet individual needs.

Job satisfaction comes with a combination of contentment and motivation. Workers need to define that combination. Leaders balance supply and demand of resources and opportunities to support workers' needs.

Worker's Balance of Contentment and Motivation Factors

Leaders can create a feasible platform of contentment and motivation factors from which workers can choose. This platform can make contentment and motivation choices very individual and tangible. Leaders and workers can collaborate on building satisfaction as dictated by the worker's autonomy of thought.

Given the autonomy of workers, it is most feasible to offer workers the opportunity to define their own contentment and motivational factors. From an organizational perspective, leaders can create a generic set of contentment and motivation factors to satisfy workers. These factors can include ratings to indicate costs. Workers can have a quota of costs allowed and then choose among the factors to match their contentment and motivational needs.

What combination of contentment and motivation makes you satisfied with yourself, your job, and your organization?

Putting workers in charge of their own contentment and motivation reinforces their autonomy, including their development and growth aspirations.

Assessing Satisfaction Factors

Satisfaction can be hard to assess. It can be determined and assessed by individuals in their unique ways. It combines contentment and motivation and is dependent upon individual scenarios of life and work. In any given year, contentment might be a priority, while motivation might take that priority in the next year.

As autonomous workers, individuals can design their own criteria for assessing their contentment and for motivation.

Inquiries might include the following:

- Do you feel satisfied with your job?
- What does satisfaction mean to you?
- Is contentment or motivation more important to you?
- What does contentment mean to you?
- What does motivation mean to you?
- What might add to your contentment, motivation, or satisfaction?
- What is the context by which you have chosen contentment and motivation factors for your satisfaction?

Managers may add to this assessment by stating their own perspectives and requirements for minimal contentment and motivation for each worker. Building satisfaction works in both directions and should be considered from both perspectives. Worker satisfaction is only relevant as it relates to organizational satisfaction. Organizational satisfaction only works if workers are satisfied, as well.

Checking the Artifacts of Your Narrative

Workers can define the artifacts of their own satisfaction. Autonomous workers have the agency to define their own needs for contentment and motivation, the ability to see options for meeting satisfaction, and take control of the work needed to build their contentment, motivation, and satisfaction. Leaders can ensure that the resources and environment are available for workers to be satisfied as they have defined it for themselves.

Organizations that have satisfied workers systematically develop, grow, and thrive. They are considered good places to work. They provide opportunities for workers to thrive.

Are workers in your organization positive when talking about their work? Do they have good stories to tell? Or are they often negative about an experience or assigned work?

Asking workers to identify artifacts of their contentment and motivation is a good approach to understanding their feelings. Also, assessing the outcomes of their work, both in their routine work and their innovative projects, will identify artifacts of high performance, development, and growth.

Basic artifacts of contentment might include the quality of routine work, while artifacts of motivation might be the continuous search for new opportunities. Consistency of attendance and diligence are artifacts of contentment. Curiosity is a great artifact of motivation. Finally, the retention of workers and positive relationships with supervisors are artifacts of contentment, and frequent promotion of workers is an artifact of motivation.

Another artifact of an autonomous organization is leaders' high priority on serving workers. Decisions are weighted heavily to promote the well-being and development of workers.

Workers, leaders, and the organization agree on factors and levels of contentment, motivation, and satisfaction. All of these artifacts together create a narrative of the organization.

> *How does your organization tell your story on the satisfaction of and with your workers? How do workers and leaders tell that story? How do outsiders tell your story?*

Chapter Summary

This final chapter includes a simple method to think about workers' mindsets, autonomy, and satisfaction. Analysis includes how you build and manage autonomy, development, and growth for worker satisfaction. Autonomy enables a combined and balanced focus on contentment and motivation factors that leads to job satisfaction. Contentment, motivation, and satisfaction are the choice of every autonomous worker.

Make your choices well!

Glossary

These terms are uniquely defined in the context of developing an autonomous environment to support autonomous work and workers.

A

Accelerated trends—society or business occurrences that align to a common thread

Adaptive—adjusting actions to accommodate a countering force or need

Advocacy—monitor and support of a mode of work or value to be applied to work

Agency—the ability to take initiative in leading a project or to solve a problem

Archetype workflows—models of common work patterns and their results, giving insight into potential causes or correlations of a missed result

Artifact—a tangible sign of a goal, a value, a belief, or mode of work

Attributes—descriptors of the components of an individual, a group, an organization, or an artifact

Autonomous skills—the ability to be independent and dependent in taking charge of one's work, decisions, and results

Autonomous worker—a person who works autonomously

Autonomy— having agency, seeing options, and the ability to be in control, to be independent, and to recognize dependence for complementary skills or knowledge

Awareness—continuous observation and acknowledgment of relevant factors or occurrences

B

Behavioral economists—economists who study the source and impact of decision behaviors on economic factors

Behavioral tendencies—the behaviors that describe an individual or group's tendencies or rationale for decision making

Behaviors—individual and group actions

Beliefs—opinions, assumptions, and biases regarding a specific subject, individual, or group

Beliefs and mode of work alignment—beliefs that drive various modes of work

Benefits/impact summary—summary chart for tracking progress as it impacts an individual or an organization

Biases, implicit and explicit—implicit beliefs that are unconscious; explicit beliefs that are conscious and intentional

Bloom's taxonomy of seven levels of thinking—incrementally defined thinking for expanding awareness and understanding of the factors leading to value creation, including remembering, understanding, applying, analyzing, synthesizing, evaluating, and creating

Brain change (Lakoff)—brains change when learning occurs

Brain steering—unlimited considerations of all domains for ideation

Brainstorming—limited considerations of a specific domain for ideation

C

Celebration—congratulatory practices, recognition, or reward for new value creation

Choice architectures—decision choices that facilitate an individual's ability to decide

Cointrapreneuring—multiple individuals working together within an organization to find efficiencies or new value

Collaboration—individuals or groups working together toward a common goal

Common community mindset (CCM)—a group of people (at least two) who work together and have agreed to a common platform of mindset components to guide their joint work

Communication models: politician, preacher, prosecutor, scientist—various approaches to communicating with others

Communications strategy: readiness, relevance, reinforcement, reflection—stages of incremental communication that facilitate collaborators' understanding and engagement

Community mentality—common goals, values, beliefs, and modes of work of a group that incent like-behaviors from members of the group

Compassion—understanding, relating, and sympathy for another's misfortune or condition from one's own experiences

Confirmation—the need to validate an individual's current belief

Connecting goals and values—the agreement of goals and values to support resulting behaviors

Conservative—a sense of individual self-sufficiency and responsibility, free markets, and privatization

Consumption chain—an individual's or an organization's connections to all areas of consuming or distributing

Contentment—a feeling of physical well-being and satisfaction

Contextual links—an individual's or organization's background factors that provide understanding of behaviors and decisions

Control—having the agency to find options to solve problems with inquiry, research, and relevant decisions

Conversation starters—facilitators for engaging in conversations that build trust and relationships

Corporate social responsibility (CSR)—the relegation of responsibility to corporations for contributing to solutions for social issues

Culture—the mindset and environment within which one lives

D

Data analysis—descriptive, exploratory, inferential, predictive, causal, mechanistic, and regressive for responding to related inquiry

Data collection—collecting data and information that is relevant to an issue or inquiry, such as brainstorming or brain steering

Decision influencers—data and/or information that sheds new light on a decision point

Decision making—actions and behaviors that lead to an action or result

Decision rationale—background/mindset thinking that drives a decision

Demand—the level of product or service that a buyer is willing to acquire

Desired outcomes—the intended and optimal, per individual perspective/mindset, results of actions and behaviors

Demand shifters—an influencer to the level of product or service that a buyer is willing to acquire

Destiny—one's personal vision for life achievement

Digital nervous system—system that provides data and information to support relevant data analysis

E

Economic analysis—inquiry into economic factors of supply and demand, opportunity costs, production possibilities, and externalities to quantify options

Emotional analysis—inquiry into mindset of all stakeholders as it relates to the mindset and decisions of a project

Entitlement—belief that an individual or organization is owed something without earning it

Entrepreneuring—the pursuit of ideation and new value within a global and external context

Environment—the conditions that surround a situation or organization

Equilibrium—a state in which levels of supply and demand meet

Experiences—all life's events and activities that create a frame for mindset development

F

Five whys—sequential analysis of events, trends, activities, or decisions that create understanding of causal, correlating, and contributing factors to a situation

Flow of thinking—extremely consuming and effective state of thinking that enables complete focus on one's work

G

Generational thinking—varying age groups with different values and beliefs that influence thinking

Generative—creating new opportunities through a countering force or need

Giver, taker, matcher—descriptions of behaviors and outcomes of individuals who consistently and continuously give, take, or match contributions when working with others

Global value dimensions—a set of values that are consistently held throughout the world to varying degrees within each nation

Goal categories—goals in personal, professional, community, and expertise domains

Goals—aspirations for achievement in support of one's vision and the pursuits to support that vision

Growth—measured progress toward a goal

H

Heuristics—activity that follows previous rationale without consideration of new circumstances

Hierarchy of goals—incremental sequence of goals that support and lead to mastery of an ultimate goal

Human development system (Maslow)—five stages of development based on human physical, social, and mastery needs

Hygiene/contentment—physical needs satisfied within job conditions

I

Idea box—freely accessible repository for anyone's idea that has been quantified and qualified according to preliminary and defined protocols

Idealized design—a design that includes forecasting of future needs

Independent, dependent, interdependent—modes of work that integrate to support autonomous activity and environments

Individual autonomy—the individual's mastery of the characteristics of autonomy

Inquiry—a continuous interest and questioning an issue of surrounding activity, decisions, and causes

Intangible decision factors/shifters—qualitative factors based in mindset values and beliefs that influence decisions

Integration of operations—awareness and understanding of how operational input and outcome impact each other

Intentionality—awareness and delivery of chosen actions and decisions

Intrapreneuring—the pursuit of ideation and new value within an organization

Invisible capital—one's connections, experiences, and subsequent knowledge that enhance one's skills, capabilities, and resources

J

Journaling—the practice of recording and reflecting on current occurrences for later considerations

K

Knowledge economy—the economic state in which knowledge as a resource is most important as it guides the use of other resources of land, labor, and capital

L

Learning—structured inquiry, research, analysis, and conclusion for new value creation

Learning context—the situation to be evaluated and the background mindsets that will shape activity and decisions

Learning and performance—learning activities that support achieving a goal, which is performance-based

Learning mindset—one's goals, values, beliefs, and modes of work that are aligned to continuous, consistent, and comprehensive learning

Learning modes—eight learning styles, including linguistic, logical/ mathematical, spatial, bodily kinesthetic, musical, interpersonal, intrapersonal, and naturalist

Learning organization—an organization that is focused on learning to support development and growth

Learning system—six steps that ensure learning, including mindset awareness, entrepreneurial options, economic quantification, emotional/mindset qualification, project implementation, and reflection

Legacy—one's professional goals for achievement

Levels of influence—stakeholders with differing levels of interest, influence, and impact on one's work, prioritizing levels of attention needed

Liberal—free-spirited wide views, and supportive of individual and community rights

Listening—a focus on a message in its completeness, including words, tone, body language, and rationale

M

Management theories X, Y, Z—theories that guide the management of employees for optimal productivity and performance, giving various levels and types of guidance for completing assigned work

Maslow's five levels of needs and development—physiological, security, belonging, esteem, and self-actualization to be achieved in sequence

Matching mindset components—aligning mindset components of goals, values, beliefs, and modes of work to ensure complementary and not conflicting work activities or decisions

Measures—tools used to track progress toward a metric goal

Mental models—values, beliefs, protocols, and paradigms that shape thinking and decisions

Mentoring—using expertise to foster awareness and development of a less experienced colleague

Metrics—the relevant measurement to define a desired outcome of goal achievement

Mind mapping—systematic practice of joining and aligning considerations and options identified during brainstorming and brain steering activities

Mindful presence—awareness of one's own and others' mindsets and needs

Mindset—what one thinks, how one thinks, why one thinks what one thinks, as manifested in one's goals, values, beliefs, and mode of work, leading to one's narrative

Mindset awareness—observation and understanding of your own and other's goals, values, beliefs, and mode of work

Mindset components—goals, values, beliefs, and mode of work

Mindset source—elements of life that have formed one's mindset, including nature and nurture, strengths, experiences, community mentality, and uncertainties of life

Mission—the pursuit of projects, work, and goals that support the pursuit of one's vision

Mode of work—the practices and protocols that guide one's work individually and with others, should be influenced by goals, values, and beliefs

Motivation—attractive opportunities to individuals to develop and grow

N

Narrative—the story of oneself, held by oneself and by others

Narrative, intended versus actual—intended narrative is desired; actual narrative is other's perspectives

Nature—the mindset cause that is derived by birth

Neural mirrors—the response messaging that communicates what the messenger conveyed, seen in facial expressions

Nurture—the mindset cause that is derived from the upbringing one receives

O

Observing others—a vehicle for understanding others and for insights into one's own activities, behaviors, decisions, their causes, and the perceptions of others

Opinions and assumptions—one's biases based on mindset causes, not factual but subjective in nature

Organizational autonomy—the organizational environment setup for learning and support of autonomous workers

Organizational profile—description of an organization's mindset, including goals, values, beliefs, and mode of work as context that sets the environment for knowledge workers

Original research—surveys, conversations, interviews, and so on that are designed to collect very specific and genuine data and information regarding a scenario or stakeholder mindset and needs

P

Pandemic of 2020—the covid-19 infectious condition that caused isolation to eliminate spread among members of society

Partners—external collaborators and stakeholders with whom one works

Performance—the achievement of an individual or organizational goal, incremental or ultimate

Persistence—the ability to persevere through obstacles, gaps, and lack of support to continue efforts toward an ultimate goal

Personal mastery—achievement of an individual's expertise of a selected domain of skills and/or knowledge

Potential for success—belief that the capacity for achieving success is universal

Predictive—foreseeing and forecasting future conditions, events, trends, and decisions

Prescriptive—directing activity toward a goal

Prioritizing stakeholders—investing in engagement based on level of influence (see above)

Productivity—level of individual achievement toward an individual goal

Profiling—describing the complete mindset of someone, including sources of mindset components and development planning

Progress tracking—recording work and value created by that work

Project charter—defining document to guide all actions, communications, and decisions within a project

Project mindset—the goals, values, beliefs, and mode of work needed for a project to be successful

Project plan—the plan that guides implementation of a project to achieve a result

Projects—structured and sequential work toward a goal that includes mindset considerations

Protocols—behavioral expectations on how work will be done within an organization or an individual's perspectives, using tools and techniques

Q

Queries—relevant inquiry into how, what, when, where, and who about a situation, obstacle, issue, or unexpected success

Quiet committing—managers commit to engaging and supporting workers who may have quietly quitted

Quiet quitting—workers disengaged from work, doing the minimum needed to fulfill job requirements

R

Recognition—calling attention to a desired activity, behavior, or decision to reinforce its continuance

Reflection—in hindsight: reviewing activities, behaviors, and outcomes for new learning

Reflections team—a team focused on review and discussion of all work and potential opportunities

Remote work—workers fulfill their job responsibilities from locations other than the organization's common office space

Reskilling—job training to support motivated workers who need additional skills for a new job or advancement

Rethinking—awareness of the need to pause for reconsideration of a heuristic or other response to a situation or need

Rewards—giving a tangible and earned gift to reward a desired activity, behavior, or decision to reinforce its continuance

S

Satisfaction and motivation—satisfaction is a minimal requirement for employment retention, and motivation instigates forward thinking, growth, and new value creation

Self-actualization—the highest level of personal mastery in which individuals use their expertise to create new value

Self-sufficiency—the ability to take control of one's self to direct activities, behaviors, and decisions in one's best interest as aligned to goals and values

Seven frames of opportunity by Drucker—seven opportunities to consider when intrapreneuring or entrepreneuring, including unexpected success and failures, incongruities, process need, industry and market structures, demographics, changes in perception, and new knowledge

Shared vision—organizations share their vision and mindset with workers to guide work, thinking, and results

Shareholders—the financial owners of a venture, initiative, or effort

Stakeholder communications by Jensen—communicating with consideration of audience, their needs, one's desired actions, and most feasible formatting of the message

Stakeholders—all who impact one's work in any way or degree of influence

Stakeholders' profiles—descriptions of stakeholders, their mindsets, mindset sources, and needs

Status quo—the application of heuristics in decision making

Strengths—what one is very good at naturally, an intuitive ability

Succession planning—advancement plan within an organization to prepare future workers to fill advanced positions

Supply—the level of product or service that a seller is willing and able to provide to a demander

Supply chain—the cycle of supply and demand that is continuous

Supply shifters—an influencer to the level of product or service that a seller is willing to sell

Surviving—work to ensure that an individual or an organization does not perform below needed levels for sustainment

Systems—cycle of workflow that integrates and influences inputs, outputs, and outcomes

System 1, reactionary response—actions, behaviors, and decisions that are immediate and do not consider options, usually based on a heuristic approach

System 2, consideration and reaction—actions, behaviors, and decisions that are not spontaneous, allowing time for consideration and evaluation of relevant queries and factors that impact the response

Systems thinking—awareness and observation of cycles of workflow and its influence to project work

T

Tangible decision factors/shifters—quantitative factors based in economic logic that influence decisions

Taxonomy (Bloom's)—series of inquiries of increasing complexity that seek to guide and clarify the value of research outcomes

Team charter—plan that clarifies a team's purpose, desired results, and mindset components that guide the work of members

Team learning—the structured processes and protocols that guide a team to observe and maximize its learning during and through work

Thriving—the intent, plan, and ability to sustain, develop, and grow

Tools—structures that facilitate inquiry, analysis, and research

Techniques—defined mode of work to use tools and protocols of communication, analysis, decision making, and planning

Trends and events—global, national, regional, and local externalities that need monitoring and awareness for potential options and opportunities for growth

Trust—solid value and belief in the credibility, validity, and reliability of a person, tool, technique, or protocol

Trust building—an intentional endeavor for building stakeholdership

U

Uncertainties—all unpredictable, unprecedented, and shocking conditions that impact one's life and sustainability

User—a person or entity that will benefit from the implementation of a tool, technique, or protocol

V

Value dimensions (Hofstede)—group of values uncovered through worldwide research as common to all people, including a rating of their importance to each group

Values—the core principles by which one lives his life

Values and goals alignment—values and goals are complementary, support each other, and are usually thought of together; see connecting goals and values above

Vision—the destiny and legacy plans that one creates for oneself

W

Workflow/archetype analysis—study of actual inputs, outcomes, and expectations to uncover obstacles, gaps, and opportunities for greater effectiveness and/or efficiencies

References

Abrams, J. and A. Burton. July 2023. "The Missing Ingredient to Achieving Peak Workplace Productivity Is Often Trust." *Fortune CHRODaily*.

Ackoff, R. 1999. "A Lifetime of Systems Thinking." *Systems Thinker Pegasus Communications*. thesystemsthinker.com. Accessed July 2024.

Ackoff, R.L. and D. Greenberg. 2008. *Turning Learning Right Side Up*. Upper Saddle River, NJ: FT Press, Wharton School Publishing.

Ackoff, R.L., J. Magidson, and H.J. Addison. 2008. *Idealized Design Creating an Organization's Future*. Upper Saddle River, NJ: Prentice Hall.

Andersen, J. 2021. *The LEGO Story How a Little Toy Sparked the World's Imagination*. New York: Mariner News.

Ariely, D. 2009. *Predictably Irrational*. New York: HarperCollins Publishers.

Ariely, D. 2011. *The Upside of Irrationality: The Unexpected Benefits of Defying Logic*. New York: Harper Perennial.

Armstrong, P. 2010. *Bloom's Taxonomy*. Nashville, TN: Vanderbilt University Center for Teaching.

Bailey, C., M. Lips-Wiersma, A. Madden, R. Yeoman, M. Thompson, and N. Chalofsky. October 2018. "The Five Paradoxes of Meaningful Work: Introduction to the Special Issue 'Meaningful Work': Prospects for the 21st Century." *Journal of Management Studies* 56 (3).

Bell, D. 1971. *The Coming of Post-Industrialist Society*. New York: Basic Books.

Berry, L.I. and K.D. Seltman. 2008. *Management Lessons From Mayo Clinic*. United States of America: McGraw Hill.

Brooks, D. March 2024a. "Resist the Pull of 'Us vs. Them' Thinking." *The New York Times*.

Brooks, D. April 2024b. "The Quiet Magic of Middle Managers." *The New York Times*.

Buruma, I. 2024. "The 17th-Century Heretic We Could Really Use Now." *The New York Times*.

Cane, A. January 2005. "The Chips Are Up at IBM: CORPORATE SCIENTISTS." *The Financial Times*.

Case, A. and A. Deaton. 2020. *Death by Despair and the Future of Capitalism*. Princeton: Princeton University Press.

Choong, K.K. and P.W. Leung. 2022. "A Critical Review of the Precursors of the Knowledge Economy and Their Contemporary Research: Implications for the Computerized New Economy." *Journal of the Knowledge Economy*.

Cline, H., R.E. Bennett, R.C. Kershaw, and B. Stecher. 1985. *The Electronic Schoolhouse: The IBM Secondary School Computer Education Program.* Hillsdale, NJ: L. Erlbaum Associates.

Davenport, T. and J. Kim. 2013. "Keeping Up With the Quants." *HBR Guide to Data Analytics Basics for Managers.* Boston: Harvard Business Review Press.

Dixon, T. and J. O'Mahony. 2023. *Pearson Economics II The Market Economy, 2023.* Victoria: Pearson Australia.

Drucker, P. 1985. *Innovation and Entrepreneurship.* New York: HarperCollins Publishers, Inc.

Duckworth, A. 2016. *Grit: The Power of Passion and Perseverance.* New York: Scribner,

Fortune. 2023. "CHRO Daily." https://fortune.com/topic/chro-daily.

Frankel, J. 2023a. *The Intentional Mindset: Data, Decisions, and Your Destiny.* New York: Business Expert Press.

Frankel, J. September 2023b. Interview by Karen Mangia. Podcast. "Quiet Committing: Jane Frankel. The Five Commitments High Impact Leaders Make and Keep to Themselves Daily." *Authority Magazine.*

Free Exchange. 2023. "Why Economics Does Not Understand Business." *The Economist.*

Friedman, T. 2016. *Thank You for Being Late.* New York: Farrar, Straus and Giroux.

Gates, B. 1999. *Business @The Speed of Thought.* New York: Warner Books, Inc.

Grant, A. 2021. *Think Again.* New York: VIKING, An imprint of Penguin Random House LLC.

Harrington, H.J. and F. Voehl. 2012. *The Organizational Master Plan Handbook.* New York: CRC Press Taylor and Francis Group.

Harter, J. September 2022. "Is Quiet Quitting Real?" *Gallup Workplace.*

Henderson, R.M. February 2018. "More and More CEOs Are Taking Their Social Responsibility Seriously." *Harvard Business Review.*

Hofstede, G., G.J. Hofstede, and M. Minkov. 2010. *Cultures and Organizations Software of the Mind.* New York: McGraw Hill.

Jensen, W. 2000. *Simplicity: The New Competitive Advantage in a World of More, Better, Faster.* New York: Basic Books.

Kahneman, D. 2011. *Thinking, Fast and Slow.* New York: Farrar, Straus and Giroux.

Kanter, R.M. May 2009. "IBM's Dynamic Workplace." *Harvard Business School Case Publications.*

Kay, J. and M. King. 2021. *Radical Uncertainty.* New York: W.W. Norton & Company, Inc.

Kelliher, C., J. Richardson, and G. Boiarintseva. September 2018. "All of Work? All of life? Reconceptualising Work-Life Balance for the 21st Century." *Human Resource Management Journal* 29 (4).

Lakoff, G. 2009. *The Political Mind*, New York: Penguin Books.

Lego.com/Discover.

Masterson, C., K. Sugiyama, and J. Ladge. 2021. "The Value of 21st Century Work-Family Supports: Review and Cross-Level Path Forward." *Journal of Organizational Behavior.*

Maurer, R. 2019. "Worker Training Needs a Common Metric." *Society of Human Resource Management HRNews.*

McGraw, T. 2007. *Prophet of Innovation.* Cambridge, MA: First Harvard University Press.

Meadows, C.J. November 2021. *Famous Business Fusions: Ideas That Revolutionized Industries* (High-Impact Business Innovation Series. 1).

Mitra, R. 2017. "Tell Me a Story: Narratives, Behaviour Change and Neuroscience." *BBC Blogs.*

Moore, J. August 2016. "What Is the Sense of Agency and Why Does It Matter?" *Frontiers in Psychology National Library of Medicine.* www.ncbi.nlm.nih.gov/pmc/articles/PMC5002400/.

Nickerson, C. 2021. "Herzberg's Motivation Two-Factor Theory." *Simply Psychology.*

Obama, B. 2006. *The Audacity of Hope.* New York: Crown First Edition.

O'Boyle, E.J. and P. Welch. 2016. "Tracing the Origins of Personalist Economics to Aristotle and Aquinas." *Forum of Social Economic* 45 (1): 3–18.

Pachceo, I. May 2023. "Nobel Laureate Robert E. Lucas, Jr., Who Transformed Macroeconomics, Dies at 85." *The Wall Street Journal.*

Pandey, S. and P. Kerni. 2015. "Analyzing the Current Trends in Learning and Development." *OPUS: HR Journal* 6 (1): 58.

Powell, W. and K. Snellman. 2004. "The Knowledge Economy." *Annual Reviews.*

PRNewswire. May 2012. "The Incredible Disappearing Office: New Technology, Tighter Budgets, and Evolving Culture Bring Telework into the Mainstream." *The Conference Board.*

Quchi, W. 1981. *Theory Z: How American Business Can Meet the Japanese Challenge.* New York: Basic Books.

Rabb, C. 2010. *Invisible Capital.* Oakland, CA: Berrett-Kohler Publishers.

Sachs, H. 2022. *What Is Theory X and Theory Y, What Is the Practical Application of Theory Y Approach to Management, The Benefits of Managers Using the Theory Y Management Style to Manage Employees, and the Problems With Managers Using the Theory X Management Style.* Middletown, Delaware.

satellinstitute.org

Schumpeter, J. 1934. *The Theory of Economic Development.* Boston: Harvard University Press.

Senge, P.M. 1990. *The Fifth Discipline.* New York: Doubleday A Division of Bantam Doubleday Dell Publishing Group.

Serrat, O. 2009. *The Five Whys Technique*. Manila, Philippines: Asian Development Bank.

Siu, E. March 2024. "Majority of Women Have Never Asked for a Raise. Here's How to Negotiate for a Higher Salary." Dayforce. www.cnbc.com/2024/03/08/most-women-dont-ask-for-a-raise-how-to-negotiate-for-higher-salary.html.

Smith, L. 2017. *Meet Maslow*. Middletown, DE: Make Profits Easy LLC.

Thaler, R. and C. Sunstein. 2009. *Nudge*. New York: Penguin Books.

Wargo, D. 2024. *Interview by J. Frankel*.

Zahidi, S. 2023. "The Future of Jobs Report 2023." *World Economic Forum*.

Zynga, A. 2014. "A Social Brain Is a Smarter Brain." *Harvard Business Review*.

About the Author

Jane Frankel is the Managing Principal of The Art of Performance LLC, which she founded in 2007. Frankel has been an advocate of lifelong learning throughout her career as a teacher, organizational design specialist, and program developer in both the private and public sectors. Her focus is on building twenty-first century innovation and learning cultures through workforce and customer engagement, strategic alliances, internships, and innovation planning. Frankel has developed multiple innovation programs requiring the collaboration of diverse mindsets. These programs include a customized curriculum to serve diverse audience needs and capabilities, customer service aligned to customer needs and mindsets, strategic partnerships with external experts for new product and services development and delivery, mentor structures for project design and implementation, project-based internships between the emerging workforce and external employers for job placement, and a Knowledge Work Institute (LinkedIn platform) to socialize the needs and uses of knowledge for its impact among social media audiences.

Frankel holds an MS degree in Organizational Dynamics from the University of Pennsylvania and an MS in Education from Temple University, both in Philadelphia, PA. She has authored *The Intentional Mindset: Data, Decisions, and Your Destiny* in 2023 and *Building an Autonomous Environment: For Yourself and Your Organization*, to be published in 2025.

Index

www.ingramcontent.com/pod-product-compliance
Lightning Source LLC
Chambersburg PA
CBHW061157220326
41599CB00025B/4519